Praise for
Be Your Future Self Now

"Knowing your Future Self is key to living powerfully and purposefully. Dr. Benjamin Hardy has laid out the groundwork and science so that you can not only know your Future Self intimately, but you can also transform your life."

—**Tony Robbins**, #1 *New York Times*
best-selling author of *Life Force*

THE SCIENCE OF
INTENTIONAL TRANSFORMATION

BE YOUR FUTURE SELF NOW

DR. BENJAMIN HARDY

HAY HOUSE, INC.
Carlsbad, California • New York City
London • Sydney • New Delhi

Published in the United States by: Hay House, Inc.: www.hayhouse .com® • **Published in Australia by:** Hay House Australia Pty. Ltd.: www .hayhouse.com.au • **Published in the United Kingdom by:** Hay House UK, Ltd.: www.hayhouse.co.uk • **Published in India by:** Hay House Publishers India: www.hayhouse.co.in

Project editor: Melody Guy
Indexer: JS Editorial, LLC
Cover design: Ploy Siripant
Interior design: Joe Bernier
Interior photos/illustrations: Gapingvoid Culture Design

Cataloging-in-Publication Data is on file at the Library of Congress

Tradepaper ISBN: 978-1-4019-7401-5
E-book ISBN: 978-1-4019-6758-1
Audiobook ISBN: 978-1-4019-6759-8

11 10 9 8 7 6 5 4 3 2
1st edition, June 2022
2nd edition, August 2023

Printed in the United States of America

This product uses papers sourced from responsibly managed forests. For more information, see www.hayhouse.com.

For my family:
Philip Hardy and Susan Knight
Trevor and Jacob Hardy
Lauren Hardy
Kaleb, Jordan, Logan, Zorah, Phoebe, and Rex

ALSO BY DR. BENJAMIN HARDY

The Gap and the Gain: The High Achievers' Guide to Happiness, Confidence, and Success (with Dan Sullivan)*

Who Not How: The Formula to Achieve Bigger Goals through Accelerating Teamwork (with Dan Sullivan)*

Personality Isn't Permanent: Break Free from Self-Limiting Beliefs and Rewrite Your Story

Willpower Doesn't Work: Discover the Hidden Keys to Success

*Available from Hay House
Please visit:

Hay House USA: www.hayhouse.com®
Hay House Australia: www.hayhouse.com.au
Hay House UK: www.hayhouse.co.uk
Hay House India: www.hayhouse.co.in

CONTENTS

Introduction: Psychology's 180 Degree Revolution xi

PART 1: 7 Threats to Your Future Self 1

Threat #1:   Without hope in your future,
               your present loses meaning 7

Threat #2:   A reactive narrative about your past
               stunts your future..15

Threat #3:   Being unaware of your environment
               creates a random evolution..............................23

Threat #4:   Being disconnected from your Future Self
               leads to myopic decisions..................................31

Threat #5:   Urgent battles and small goals keep you
               stuck 37

Threat #6:   Not being in the arena is
               failing by default 45

Threat #7:   Success is often the catalyst for failure 51

Conclusion: Future Self threats 59

PART 2: 7 Truths about Your Future Self 61

Truth #1:   Your future drives your present 69

Truth #2:   Your Future Self is different than you expect 77

Truth #3:   Your Future Self is the Pied Piper.........................85

Truth #4:   The more vivid and detailed your Future Self,
               the faster you'll progress 95

Truth #5:   Failing as your Future Self is better than
               succeeding as your current self..........................101

Truth #6:   Success is achieved by being true
               to your Future Self, nothing else 109

Truth #7:   Your view of God impacts your Future Self........113

Conclusion: Future Self truths..123

PART 3: 7 Steps for Being Your Future Self 125

Step #1:   Clarify your contextual purpose 129

Step #2:   Eliminate lesser goals 141

Step #3:   Elevate from needing to wanting to knowing.... 149

Step #4:   Ask for exactly what you want............................157

Step #5:   Automate and systemize your Future Self 163

Step #6:   Schedule your Future Self 169

Step #7:   Aggressively complete imperfect work 175

Conclusion: Future Self steps...183

Conclusion: Be Your Future Self Now 185

Endnotes...189

Index 203

Acknowledgments 210

About the Author 212

"To be, or not to be? That is the question."
— William Shakespeare, *Hamlet*

PSYCHOLOGY'S 180 DEGREE REVOLUTION

"Assume the consciousness of being the one you want to be,
and you will be saved from your present state."

—Neville Goddard[1]

On the evening of October 4, 2015, instead of studying for his 11th-grade history test, 17-year-old Jimmy Donaldson filmed four YouTube videos.

While Jimmy had been actively creating YouTube videos for over three years, these recordings were different. Rather than doing commentaries on video games or discussing the lives and incomes of famous YouTubers as he normally did, Jimmy invited his audience to sit-in on the intimate and vulnerable conversations he had *with himself.*

In the first segment, Jimmy spoke to his Future Self, 6 months into the future.

In the second video, he talked to his Future Self, 12 months into the future.

In the third recording, he addressed his Future Self, 5 years into the future.

And in the fourth, he spoke to his Future Self, 10 years into the future.

Each video lasted around two minutes.

Nothing crazy.

But in those pivotal moments, Jimmy was completely raw and honest about what he wanted, and what he expected, of his Future Self.

Rather than publishing these videos immediately as he normally would, he scheduled each clip to publish in the future—exactly 6 months, 12 months, 5 years, and 10 years respectively from October 4, 2015.

Six months later, on April 4, 2016, the first video went live on Jimmy's YouTube channel.[2]

The video began with Jimmy showing his computer screen and highlighting the current stats of his You-Tube channel.

"At the time I'm filming this video, I have 8,000 subscribers and 1.8 million views. So, whenever you see this, compare these numbers to whatever I have when you watch this."

He then has a short conversation with his Future Self.

"What would I want to say to me in six months? Hopefully you're still uploading daily. Hopefully you have at least 15,000 subscribers, future me. That would be embarrassing if I don't, then you guys (speaking to his audience) would be like, um, yeah . . . As of now, I'm still enjoying YouTube. Hopefully future me still enjoys it. It would be crazy if I had some ridiculous amount of subscribers, like 20K or something, in six months."

Not only did Jimmy achieve his 6-month goal, but by the time his 12-month *Future Me* video released on October 4, 2016, Jimmy had increased his subscribers tenfold since his 6-month future me video went live—he now had over 200,000 subscribers.

He consistently made videos viewed by millions.

His videos grew bolder and more innovative.

He fully embraced the brand of his alter ego—*MrBeast*.

The creation of his future me videos became a turning-point in Jimmy's life. These candid conversations marked a crucial inflection point when Jimmy got courageous toward his dreams. Within a few years, he made hundreds of millions of dollars as the fastest rising internet sensation, *ever*.

MrBeast's psychology and commitment shifted that night he skipped his history test to go public about his Future Self. You can actually see a clear distinction from Jimmy's videos pre and post October 2015. He filmed himself less often behind the screen playing video games and more often in front of the camera. He pumped the MrBeast concept and brand and recruited friends who became common features in his videos to support the MrBeast ideology.

On June 1, 2016, his first video went super viral, garnering more than 20 million views. He and his friends were shown commenting on the best YouTube introductions. The episode had more visual effects, and MrBeast himself had more confidence and swagger.[3]

Days later, he introduced his growing style of doing either interesting stunts or ridiculous feats. He bought an outdoor picnic table and cut the whole thing in half, using only plastic butter knives. He spent more than $60 to purchase thousands of plastic knives to accomplish the task that took dozens of hours to do. That video received more than three million views.[4]

On August 23, 2016, MrBeast garnered two million views of his friend wrapping him in 100 rolls of saran wrap.[5]

On October 16, 2016, he published a skit of himself pretending that every online ad he read immediately became real.[6] "Win a free iPad" became a new iPad that all-of-a-sudden appeared on his doorstep. "Have your laptop run 100 times faster" instantly produced a new laptop in his lap. Following a running commentary with jokes, the adventure ended when he and his friends destroyed the computers used in the video.

That video got MrBeast another nine million views.

On January 8, 2017, MrBeast livestreamed himself counting to 100,000.[7] The feat took almost 40 hours and resulted in over 20 million views. A month later he counted to 200,000, and then to 300,000.[8,9]

In August of 2017, he filmed himself saying "Logan Paul" 100,000 times.[10]

As his stunts became more ridiculous and absurd, Jimmy evolved into his desired Future Self. His experimentation became bolder. He developed donation videos as a staple of his growing brand.

On June 15, 2017, he published a video of himself giving $10,000 to a homeless man.[11] Later, he gave $1,000 to 10 different homeless people.[12]

On August 15, 2017, he filmed himself donating $10,000 to random Twitch Streamers—people who play video games publicly on the internet.[13]

His donation videos highlighted the hysterical reactions of the people who received large amounts of money unexpectedly.

On August 23, 2017, Jimmy published a video of himself tipping pizza delivery guys $10,000, and laughing at their overwhelm.[14] He hugged an older man who spoke through his tears about how much the money would impact him and his wife.

On August 30, 2017, Jimmy tipped Uber drivers $10,000.[15]

In addition to donating larger and larger sums of money—which he originally got from various sponsors of his videos—MrBeast performed bigger stunts and games where people could win greater sums of money.

He tested how many balloons were needed to lift him off the ground, drove more than 100 hours to purchase a Snickers bar from every Walmart in his state, bought a car with only pennies, and gave three million pennies to the person who became his three millionth subscriber.[16,17,18,19]

By October 4, 2020, when his third future me video aired, MrBeast had become the fastest rising YouTuber on the internet.

He had more than 40 million subscribers.

He'd become a household name.

He operated a business with a team of more than 30 people and an annual revenue in excess of $100 million.

His videos averaged 30 million views—some with hundreds of millions of views.

A little more contemplative than his 6- and 12-month videos, Jimmy's *Hi Me In 5 Years* recording showed a 17-year-old Jimmy connected with a much different and bigger Future Self.

> Right now, I'm in high school. When you see this, I will be in, uh . . . I'm not even going to be in college. This is going to be after college. Wow. Dude. This is going to be *crazy*!

The wheels in his head seemed to spin.

It's 2015 for me right now. Dude, what if I'm dead?

The thought visibly terrifies him. He covers his mouth as if to stop the words. His eyes widen. Looking frightened, he continues.

Oh, that would be weird. That would be so weird. RIP (rest in peace). Dude that would be really weird.

After contemplating the potential that he could be dead when this video goes live on his YouTube channel, he grows serious about his Future Self.

If I don't have 1,000,000 subscribers when you see this video, my entire life has been a failure. I hope I have a million subs . . . *I better have a million subs!*

His conviction heightens.

Then, the weight of realizing his dream overwhelms him. Jimmy sits back in his chair, caught up in his thinking. He lets out an outward breath that flitters his hair.

Dude, that would be . . .

He can't finish his own sentence.

He shakes his head and closes his eyes, contemplating desperately and deeply what he wants. He shakes his head and gazes at his bedroom ceiling. He connects so deeply with his desired Future Self that he forgets he's filming.

After a moment of imagination, he continues his conversation with his camera.

> I don't even know what college I'm going to. But by the time you watch this video, I'll have finished high school, gone to college . . . probably be doing YouTube as a job. Hopefully . . . Maybe . . . Maybe . . .

He bites his hand while voicing his dream.

> Dude, I really hope I have a million subs by now. *Please future me, please.* What am I doing with my hand?

He finishes his video by proclaiming one more time:

> I better have a million subscribers when this goes public.

At the writing of this book—December of 2021—it's been a little over a year since MrBeast's *Hi Me In 5 Years* video went live.

Jimmy has more than 82 million subscribers. His stunts get bolder.

Not only did Jimmy become his desired Future Self, he shattered his vision again and again.

From an outside perspective, Jimmy's transformation over the past six years is almost unbelievable. He went from a 17-year-old kid with zero money making videos in his bedroom to being one of the most famous people in the world. Extremely wealthy and business savvy, he aspires to one day become president of the United States.

Do methodologies exist that you and I can follow to create similar results in our own lives? The exciting answer is *absolutely yes*. Recent research in psychology provides an extremely simple explanation for MrBeast's amazing transformation. You can apply the process for desired results and change in your own life.

This book will show you exactly how.

A SHIFT IN THE SCIENCE

"Much of the history of psychology has been dominated by a framework in which people and animals are driven by the past."

– Martin Seligman, et al.[20]

From the late 1800s to the late 1900s, the field of psychology focused on human problems. Referred to as *pathology*, the theories and therapies centered on alleviating problems including depression and suicide. The concept of human flourishing received little emphasis.

During this period, science suggested that human beings are the direct byproduct of their own past. This view is known as *determinism*—the idea that human behavior is simply one domino toppled by the dominos that came before.[21,22,23,24] The dominos of past events dictate who you are and what you're doing now. There is no human agency or freedom—simply stimulus and response.

In other words, according to determinism, your life today is the secondary synthesis of your past.

Although the dominant view, determinism was extremely limiting and negative. If a person had a lot of problems, those problems could only be explained by their past. And sadly, the main objective of psychology was simply to explain the problems, not solve them.

In the 1990s, a group of revolutionary psychologists who dubbed themselves "positive psychologists," questioned these central dogmas of psychology. They asked different questions and ran different types of experiments trying to better understand what led someone to be happy, healthy, and successful.

This research, along with breakthroughs in technology and neuroscience, produced a different picture about what makes a person who they are. In fact, modern research provides a near opposite explanation from previously held beliefs.

Research now shows that a person's past does not drive or dictate their actions and behaviors. *Rather, we are pulled forward by our future.*[25]

As human beings, we have a unique characteristic held by no other species on the planet. People have the ability to not only think about our own future, but to have countless potential scenarios for our future. Additionally, humans are able to contemplate deeply on our potential prospects.[26]

For example, you may have lots of potential options before you such as taking a certain job or staying where you are, moving to a different country or remaining local. We have hundreds of potential futures we could fulfill and countless decisions we could make for our lives. We think about these options and eventually make a decision about which direction we'll go.

Psychologists call this unique human ability *prospection*; as people, everything we do is driven by our prospects of the future.[27] Prospection is based on a *teleological* view of the world, which views all human action and behavior as driven by goals—whether short term or long term.[28]

From this view, *every human action has a purpose.* Another word for purpose is *goal.* All human-action is goal-driven, even if the goal of the behavior isn't consciously considered by the individual.

Take for example, walking to the refrigerator to get food. That behavior is driven by the goal of satisfying hunger, a distraction, or indulgence. Whatever the goal, that purpose is the driver behind walking to the fridge.

Going to school is another example. People go to school for a reason. Each individual student will have different goals for attending. One student may be trying to qualify for college. Another student may be there because their parents forced them, and they don't want to get in trouble. Despite having very different internal reasons for being in class, both students are there to satisfy an end.

While the student's purpose may not be conscious or inspiring, their reason still exists. Even if the goal is simply immediate gratification or escape, then doing harmful drugs or wasting away on social media are actions driven by reasons.

Some questions you could ask yourself are:

- What is the reason or goal for this activity?
- What benefit am I getting from this?
- Where is this activity taking me?

There are three levels to understanding a particular event or action:

1. The what
2. The how
3. The why

Level one is the ability to explain what happened. In this case, you could say: he went to school. That's the what.

Level two is the ability to explain how the behavior happened. In this case, you could say: he got a ride to school.

Level three is being able to explain why the behavior happened. There is always a why for everything someone does. That why is their reason or goal for what they're doing.

Knowing the why is the deepest and most powerful form of knowledge because the why is always the driver of the what and how. When you understand why the stock market goes up and down, making informed decisions about investing becomes easier. When you understand why someone does what they do, their actions and behaviors make a lot more sense.

There is always a why or goal behind human behavior. There is a purpose or reason for all human activity. The more conscious and clear you are about choosing your purpose and goals, the how begins to take care of itself. Your behavior follows your purpose and goals. Without conscious purpose, the how becomes conflicted and chaotic.

All goals or motivations fit within two categories: approach or avoid.[29,30] The reason for doing anything is either to approach something you want to happen, or to avoid something you don't want to happen. As a rule, 80 percent of people are primarily driven by fear or avoidance, while 20 percent of people are driven by approach and courage.

As Dr. David Hawkins explains:

> The advertising industry plays off our fears to sell us products. Grief has to do with the past, but fear, as we ordinarily experience it, is of the future. Fear is emotionally experienced in everyday life by the average person as worry, anxiety, or panic . . . Fear is a shrinkingness and a fear of the future.[31]

Approach motivations and avoid motivations are both goals. For instance, going to work because you don't want to lose your house is an avoidance-driven goal. Going to work to get a promotion is more approach-motivated.

Your reason or goal, whether positive or negative, approach or avoidance motivated, is the driver of your thoughts, energy, and actions.

In all instances, humans act as we do based on the future we see for ourselves. That may be a future we're trying to avoid, or a future we're trying to create. That future may be decades or seconds away.

In addition to being driven primarily by fear, the average person is mostly driven by short-term goals such as distracting themselves with social media instead of working, getting to the end of the workday, getting to the weekend, or paying the bills.

Said rapper and business mogul, 50 Cent, and author Robert Greene in *The 50th Law*:

> By our nature as rational, conscious creatures, we cannot help but think of the future. But most people, out of fear, limit their view of the future to a narrow range. Thoughts of tomorrow, a few weeks ahead, perhaps a vague plan for the months to come. We are generally dealing with so many immediate battles that it is hard for us to lift our gaze above the moment. It is a law of power, however, that the further and deeper we contemplate the future, the greater our capacity to shape it to our desires.[32]

Being driven by fear is a lower state of consciousness than being driven by courage and vision. Deep emotional development is required to transition beyond fear as your driver to levels of acceptance, courage, and love as reasons for action.

In addition to fear being a core emotional driver of human action, some psychologists believe human beings have not evolved to effectively think years or decades into the future.[33] Our hunter-gatherer ancestors weren't planning for retirement by age 65. Instead, they were strategizing for their next meal or trying to avoid being eaten.

As further proof that people struggle to think ahead, consider that the median age an American starts planning for retirement is 27. And with almost four decades to accomplish their goal, the median retirement savings totals $107,000. As great as this number sounds to a 27-year-old, that's only $310 of monthly income after retirement.

Whoops.

Speaking of age 65, another reason people likely struggle contemplating and strategizing for a long-term future is that the average human life expectancy has nearly doubled over the past 150 years. In 1860, the average life expectancy in America was 39 years old.[34] Eighty years is a long time to look ahead and plan for.

We have a lot of things working against us when it comes to living effectively. Shifting our goals from fear-based, reactive, and short term to proactive, long term, and love-based is the path to a successful and happy life. Your view of your Future Self is the compass that draws you forward.

This takes us to the growing body of research on the subjects of prospection, identity, and Future Self. Increasing numbers of psychologists are focusing their research on the importance of a person's view of their own Future Self. TED Talks by prominent psychologists are aimed at the critical importance of one's connection to and creation of their own Future Self.

Consider the themes of the following TED Talks given in recent years:

- *The psychology of your Future Self*[35]
- *The battle between your present and Future Self*[36]
- *Essential questions to ask your Future Self*[37]
- *A journey to your Future Self*[38]
- *Guidance from your Future Self*[39]
- *Saying hello to your Future Self*[40]
- *How can we help our Future Selves?*[41]
- *Thinking forward for your Future Self*[42]
- *How to make our present self become our Future Self*[43]
- *Challenge your Future Self*[44]
- *How to step into your Future Self*[45]

As the science on prospection and Future Self continues to grow and become increasingly compelling, Future Self coaching and meditation programs are in development.

Yet, there has never been a definitive book written on the topic until now. Research among psychologists is on the cutting edge, and the science is still young. The science of Future Self will increase during the next two decades. This book is here to catch you up on the latest science to this point.

In this highly practical book, you'll learn:

- the science of your Future Self
- how to connect with and create your desired Future Self
- how to expand your Future Self far, far beyond what you currently imagine, just as MrBeast instinctively did

The quality of connection you have with your own Future Self determines the quality of your life and behaviors now. Research shows that the more connected you are to your own Future Self, the wiser decisions you make here and now. Contemplating your Future Self, you're more likely to invest in and set yourself up for an abundant retirement, exercise and eat healthier, and you're less likely to engage in delinquent or self-defeating acts.[46,47,48]

The Future Self concept is simple yet rarely practiced. To make quality decisions, know where those decisions will take you. Decisions and actions are best when reverse-engineered from a desired outcome. Start with what you want and work backward. Think and act *from* your goal, rather than toward your goal. Your brain does this automatically. Indeed, neuroscientists now agree the brain is essentially a "prediction machine," guiding behavior toward the expected future.[49] Learning is the process of updating and improving our brain's predictions.[50]

The clearer you are on where you want to go, the less distracted you'll be by endless options.

When you're disconnected with your Future Self, you get caught up in urgent goals that often result in low-quality behavior in the present. For the majority, this is the norm.

Many people are primarily driven by short-term goals, which are disconnected from the long-term repercussions of those decisions. This reality is depicted in a 2010 episode of *The Simpsons*, "MoneyBart," when Homer, an irresponsible father, is confronted with his responsibilities and shirks them with alcohol.[51]

His wife, Marge, tries to get Homer back on track. "Someday, these kids will be out of the house, and you'll regret not spending more time with them."

"That's a problem for future Homer." He shakes his head. "Man, I don't envy that guy." Homer pours vodka into a mayonnaise jar, drinks the contents, and collapses of an apparent heart attack.

We laugh at Homer because we know deep down that we are the same. We may not be choosing mayonnaise and vodka over our children, but we knowingly leave problems for our Future Selves all the time.

In the 1990s, on *The Late Show with David Letterman*, the comedian Jerry Seinfeld discussed this common human plight:

> I saw an ad. I love this concept of, "No payments until June."
>
> People are like, "Oh June, it will never be June."
>
> They buy things and say to themselves, "The guy in June, he'll have money somehow."
>
> And I do that with myself.
>
> Like late at night, I think, "Well, it's night, I'm having a good time, I don't want to go to sleep.
>
> I'm Night Guy.
>
> Getting up after five hours' sleep?
>
> That's Morning Guy's problem. Let him worry about that. I'm Night Guy, I've got to party."

Then you get up after five hours of sleep, you're cranky, you're exhausted.

Night Guy always screws Morning Guy.

There's nothing Morning Guy can do to get back at Night Guy.

The only thing Morning Guy could do is try to oversleep so many times that Day Guy loses his job and then Night Guy doesn't have any more money to go out.

Letterman laughed and replied, "You have done an excellent job of crystallizing the dichotomy of modern American life."[52]

Because we're disconnected from our Future Selves, we opt for near immediate goals or dopamine hits. This short-term seeking ends up costing our Future Selves big.[53] As Harvard psychologist and Future Self researcher, Dr. Daniel Gilbert, asked, "Why do we make decisions our Future Selves will regret?"[54]

This brings up a counterintuitive but important truth— the more connected you are to your Future Self, the better you live in the present.

- It is not the past, but the future, that drives a person's actions and behaviors.

- All goals can be placed in two categories: approach or avoidance.

- Connected to your Future Self, you can appreciate, embrace, and love the present.

- Connection to your Future Self creates purpose and meaning in the present.

- The more connected you are to your longer-term Future Self, the better and wiser your decisions today.

Being connected to your Future Self makes you happy, productive, and successful.

That's the crazy part. Connection to your Future Self elevates your present self and circumstances. You truly prize the invaluable goldmine that is your life right now. Your connection to your future is how you live powerfully now.

BE YOUR FUTURE SELF NOW

Exhaustion hung over me like a cloud as I drove home from work.

On any normal day, I'd come home and relax after a long day's work. But this particular day, I'd been writing this book and thinking about the research on Future Self. How could I use what I learned to be a better husband? How could I connect with my Future Self to be a better father to my six energetic kids who would be hungry for Dad's attention when I arrived? Truthfully, I'd become aware that more often than I'd like to admit, I wasn't as engaged with my family as I wanted to be.

Once I reached my neighborhood, I pulled to the side of the road to truly contemplate who I wanted to be when I arrived home. I considered my own Future Self. Twenty years from now, I'll be 53 years old. All six of my children will be adults and no longer living at home.

Sitting in my parked car, a few roads from my house, I asked myself, "How would my Future Self feel, and what would they do, if the 53-year-old me could come back and live my life for the rest of today?"

A quote from Viktor Frankl, the Austrian psychiatrist and Holocaust survivor, came to mind:

> Live as if you were living already for the second time and as if you had acted the first time as wrongly as you are about to act now!
>
> It seems to me that there is nothing which would stimulate a man's sense of responsibleness more than this maxim, which invites him to imagine first that the present is past and, second, that the past may yet be changed and amended.[55]

I decided to give Frankl's idea a try.

I decided to live the rest of the day as if I were my Future Self, 20 years into the future, and my Future Self had the opportunity to time travel back and relive the rest of today.

When I pulled into my driveway, 3-year-old Phoebe was outside waiting.

"Daddy!" She jumped around, excited to see me.

Watching my beautiful and witty daughter, I knew my Future Self, 20 years from now, would give anything to experience this single moment.

As my Future Self, I saw this moment very differently than I normally do. I was brought to tears by how much I loved her. I recognized her as a perfect gift sent from God.

I jumped out of the car and hugged Phoebe like I hadn't seen her in 20 years. "Do you want me to chase you?"

"Yeah!" She took off, giggling.

Laughing, I chased her down the block. Scooping her into my arms, I hugged her close. *How is this my life? How am I so lucky?*

Taking in the setting, I saw my neighborhood and street differently. I felt reverence for what I experienced. I grasped that I stood on holy ground.

After playing blissfully with Phoebe for about five minutes, I snapped a selfie to always remember the time my Future Self came back and played with his little girl.

October 30, 2021, playing with Phoebe as my 53-year-old
Future Self. Photo: courtesy of the author.

Phoebe and I went inside where my older kids argued with each other as energetic and normal kids do. In the kitchen, Lauren busily made dinner while helping baby Rex and Zorah.

On a regular day, I might immediately chide or correct my older kids. I might zone out.

But on this day, with my Future Self in mind, my family felt far more important than I normally see them. Rather than being frustrated by the clutter, I *loved* the toys scattered about the house.

I loved the homeschool books and assignments strewn across the kitchen table.

I loved seeing my kids playing with each other.

My wife, Lauren—her beauty took my breath. *How the heck did I get this amazing life?*

Rather than feeling annoyed, I felt astonished by how much I loved the banter of my 10- to 14-year-old kids. To my Future Self, these three are in their 30s. What would my Future Self say if they could come back and just have five minutes? Rather than speaking, I'm confident my Future Self would want nothing more than to listen to, learn from, and affirm these incredible kids.

I pulled the proverbial cotton balls out of my ears and put them in my mouth.

I listened.
I engaged.
I laughed.
I loved.
I connected.

The seismic shift within felt elevated, evolved, and profound. Things that normally frustrated me seemed completely trivial. Totally in flow, I loved the things that often annoyed me. Not only did I feel present and engaged, but I acted with greater kindness, perspective, and wisdom. My Future Self would handle this situation differently and better than current me.

Tapping into my Future Self, and living as my Future Self changed everything.

Even deeper, I realized and fully appreciated that my Future Self might not be here in 20 years.

I could be gone. Recently, a friend's 2-year-old died in a freak and horribly tragic accident because he accidently got the cord to the window blinds wrapped around his neck. *Memento Mori* is an ancient Stoic term for keeping death always on your mind to fully value and appreciate this moment.

Sadly, I often miss the incredible moments all around me. Without a sense of purpose and mission, I fail to appreciate what's right in front of me. I fail to value the infinite worth of my current life, simply because I'm disconnected. Viktor Frankl suggests we imagine this moment has passed, forced to deal with the negative consequences of not being more conscious of what we were doing.

This is why the research on Future Self is so compelling. Being connected allows you to better comprehend and appreciate the goldmine of *this* moment, right here. Seeing your current life through the eyes of your Future Self, you see opportunities you were previously blind to. If you stay connected with your Future Self, you'll *value* your present.

What about you? If your Future Self—20 years from now—had a conversation with you, what would they say?

How would your Future Self view your current situation?

How differently would you act with your Future Self in mind?

THE PROMISE OF THIS BOOK

In the pages that follow, you're going to learn how to be your Future Self now. As your Future Self now, you can create the life you want.

MrBeast's enormous success came as the result of his commitment toward his desired Future Self. His courage led to consistent, deliberate practice, which is the systematic way to develop expertise in anything.[56,57] To do deliberate practice requires being deliberate toward a specific goal. Like MrBeast, have a clear view of your Future Self.[58]

Author and philosopher, Dr. Stephen R. Covey, said, "Mental creation always precedes physical creation."[59] Anyone who has created something substantial did so by seeing it in their mind first, then working toward the image. As they took steps forward, their vision clarified, expanded, and evolved.

Even the Bible describes, "Faith is the substance of things hoped for, the evidence of things not seen."[60] Whoever you're being, right now *is the evidence* of your Future Self. Your level of faith in and commitment toward your Future Self is evidenced by everything you do, and every thought you think.

Once you are clear and committed, everything will filter through your goal—what psychologists call *selective attention*.[61]

You see what you're looking for.

You see what you care about.

What you focus on expands.

The father of American psychology, William James, put it this way:

> Millions of items of the outward order are present to my senses which never properly enter into my experience. Why? Because they have no interest for me. My experience is what I agree to attend to.[62]

Not only do you see what you're looking for, but you act toward what you most want and have decided will be yours.

Faith is a principle of action and power.

By faith, you can move mountains, put a man on the moon, make millions, and heal impossible maladies. To exercise this level of faith, fashion a vision of what you want. In the words of American author Florence Shinn, "know you've already received and act according."[63]

- Know that whatever you want is already yours.

- Act as though everything you want can and will be yours.

The truth is, we all are already doing this right now. The challenge is to hone the future we envision for ourselves. We're being driven by our views of the future.

But why *that* particular future, the one you're currently committed to?

What if you chose something else?

What if you committed to what you truly want?

When you commit 100 percent to what you want and know the end result is already yours, there will be a growing body of evidence about the future you're creating. You'll stop associating pain with the work and changes required for your goals. Instead, you'll associate pain with not making progress toward your dreams. You'll associate pain with the short-term dopamine hits that were once your escape.

You'll be far more courageous.

You'll develop mentorships and collaborations with like-minded people.

Your mindset, beliefs, and mental models will change and you'll see the world far differently than your former self.

Your results will improve. As leadership experts Jim Dethmer, Diana Chapman, and Kaley Klemp state:

> Commitment is a statement of what "is." You can know what you're committed to by your results, not by what you say your commitments are. We are all committed. We are all producing results. The result is proof of a commitment.[64]

Your behavior will change because your identity changed. Your identity is what you're most committed to.

Your identity is based on the vision you have for yourself. When you change your committed vision, your identity immediately changes, which in turn, immediately changes the flow of your thoughts and behaviors.

Yes, it will require courage to fully embrace your Future Self.

Yes, it will sometimes take more time than you anticipated.

Yes, there will be obstacles.

But if you're committed, everything you face along the way will only better prepare you for what you truly want.

Everything that comes at you will strengthen your resolve.

You'll be able to turn any experience to your gain, moving you further and evolving you beyond what you could initially imagine.

When you're 100 percent committed and have faith, *you will find the way.* There is always a way. As Ralph Waldo Emerson said, "When you make a decision, the universe conspires to make it happen."

Like MrBeast, you can create a future radically beyond anything you can currently imagine. Like me with my daughter, Phoebe, you can immediately change old patterns, today. The first step is to decide who your Future Self will be, and BE your Future Self now.

Visit www.futureself.com to write a letter to your Future Self. Schedule the letter to return to you at certain time frames, just like MrBeast set his videos to be published at scheduled times.

Part 1 of this book breaks down the **seven biggest threats** to your Future Self.

Part 2 of this book teaches you the **seven most powerful truths** about your Future Self.

Part 3 of this book gives you the **seven specific steps to imagine, define, and be** your Future Self now.

This is the most straight-forward and science-based guide on living powerfully in the present by creating the future you want.

This book brings together ancient wisdom and cutting-edge science to explain in simple terms how you can radically change your life.

Are you ready?

Let's begin.

Cheers to your Future Self.

PART 1
FUTURE SELF THREATS

Threat #1:	Without hope in your future, your present loses meaning
Threat #2:	A reactive narrative about your past stunts your future
Threat #3:	Being unaware of your environment creates a random evolution
Threat #4:	Being disconnected from your Future Self leads to myopic decisions
Threat #5:	Urgent battles and small goals keep you stuck
Threat #6:	Not being in the arena is failing by default
Threat #7:	Success is often the catalyst for failure

(PART 1)

7 THREATS TO YOUR FUTURE SELF

"it is a peculiarity of man that he can only live by looking to the future."
—Viktor Frankl

"Hope is an essential part of the human condition. Without hope, we wither and perish."

—Seth Godin[1]

Even at a young age, Viktor Frankl was intensely curious. Drawn to helping people, he wanted to be a psychiatrist before age ten.

The middle child of three children, Viktor was born in Vienna, Austria, on March 26, 1905, to deeply devout parents. His mother, Elsa Frankl, was a tenderhearted woman from Prague known for her piety. His father, Gabriel Frankl, worked his way from a lowly government stenographer to become director of the Ministry of Social Service.

In high school, Frankl studied psychology and began correspondence with Sigmund Freud, one of the world's most influential psychologists. Frankl sent Freud a paper he wrote, which led to its publication in the International Journal of Psychoanalysis.

In 1925, a year after graduating college, Frankl preferred the thinking of Alfred Adler, another influential psychologist, who worked with Freud before the two parted ways. Adler's theories focused on community and social reform, and aimed at helping the individual overcome their own inferiority complexes to reach a stage of internal and external superiority.

During that same year, Frankl published another article that explored the frontier between psychotherapy and philosophy, focusing on the importance of meaning and values. These topics became the central subject of his life's work. While Freud and Adler emphasized a person's *past* as the central aspect of their development, Frankl focused on a person's *future* as the central aspect of their psychology. Frankl's developing theory, which he called *logotherapy* based on the Greek word *logos* for "meaning," believed a person's development and quality of their mental health, stemmed from having meanings to fulfill in their own future.

While completing his doctorate in medicine, in 1928 and 1929, Frankl organized cost-free counseling centers for teenagers in seven cities, which resulted in a significant drop in the number of student suicides. Frankl gained international attention and received invitations to join influential psychologists and universities throughout Europe.

Following graduation from medical school in 1931, Frankl served as lead doctor in charge of the ward for suicidal women at the Psychiatric Hospital at the Maria Theresien Schloessl Neurological Hospital in Vienna. In 1937, at age 32, Frankl opened his own clinic. Months later Germany invaded Austria and Frankl ran his psychiatric practice from his parent's home to avoid being caught by the Nazis.

While the director of the Neurological Department at the Rothschild Hospital for Jewish patients, he began work on his first book, *The Doctor and the Soul.* In this work, he laid out his revolutionary findings on the essential need for people to have a future purpose to be happy and healthy.[2]

In 1942, Frankl married Tilly Grosser, a nurse he'd met while working at Rothschild Hospital. He wrote his book throughout that year and Tilly became pregnant. Months after being married, Frankl and Tilly, as well as his parents, were arrested and brought to the concentration camp at Theresienstadt "Terezin Camp" in present-day Czech Republic. Six months later, his father died of starvation and exhaustion.

While in this horrific concentration camp, Frankl focused on the psychological crises pressing upon fellow prisoners and himself. In his efforts to combat the danger of suicide, Frankl worked alongside fellow inmate Regina Jonas, the world's first female rabbi, to help others find meaning in their suffering.

In 1944, Frankl and Tilly, and shortly thereafter, Frankl's 65-year-old mother, were transported to the extermination camp Auschwitz-Birkenau. His mother was immediately murdered in the gas chamber and Tilly was moved to a different camp in Bergen-Belsen. Devastated at being separated from Tilly, Frankl was transported by cattle car to the labor camps of Kaufering and Türkheim.

While at Auschwitz, Frankl's manuscript of *The Doctor and the Soul* was discovered and destroyed. Aside from his family, this manuscript was his most prized possession and the only physical item he had brought with him in the initial chaos of his arrest. Frankl had kept the manuscript hidden in his clothes and protected it with his life. Within those pages were the perspectives he used to give hope and meaning to others in their sufferings.

His utter resolve to rewrite and publish that book, as well as be reunited with his wife and family members, kept Frankl from completely losing hope. He explained:

> When I was taken to the concentration camp of Auschwitz, a manuscript of mine ready for publication was confiscated. Certainly, my deep desire to write this manuscript anew helped me to survive the rigors of the camps I was in.[3]

In 1945, Frankl contracted typhoid fever. To avoid fatal vascular collapse, he kept himself awake at night by reconstructing *The Doctor and the Soul* on slips of paper stolen from the camp office.

At last, on April 27, 1945, U.S. troops liberated the concentration camp. Anxious to find Tilly and his family members, Frankl returned to Vienna where he learned Tilly, his mother, brother, and brother's wife had all been murdered.

Devastated, Frankl found support in friends and in his determination to rewrite his book. In 1946, Frankl became director of the Vienna Neurological Policlinic, a position he held for 25 years. He completed *The Doctor and the Soul* including an additional chapter on the psychology of the concentration camp. One of the first books published in postwar Vienna, the first edition sold out within days.

Frankl spent nine days dictating his experience in the concentration camp as his most famous work, *Man's Search for Meaning*. Throughout 1946, he gave public lectures explaining his central thoughts on meaning, resilience, and the importance of embracing life even in the face of great adversity. Frankl married again, published many books, and developed his therapies based on having a meaning toward one's future.

Viktor Frankl was and is one of the most important people of the 20th century. *Man's Search for Meaning* sold tens of millions of copies, providing hope and healing to many people. In *Man's Search for Meaning*, Frankl repeatedly shared Friedrich Nietzsche's words, "He who has a why to live for can bear almost any how."

From Frankl's perspective, a clear future is essential in all circumstances and critical in trauma. The most fundamental threat to a person's Future Self is not the loss of freedom but the absence of purpose and meaning.

Frankl's story provides a startling illustration of how serious these threats can be. Lose the purpose for your future and you die in the present.

WITHOUT HOPE IN YOUR FUTURE, YOUR PRESENT LOSES MEANING

"Your vision of where or who you want to be is the greatest asset you have. Without having a goal it's difficult to score."

—Paul Arden[4]

While in the camps, Frankl could predict with extreme accuracy when a fellow inmate would die.

Once purpose was extinguished in a fellow prisoner, Frankl watched as the glow of life left their eyes. No longer willing to share their small piece of daily bread, they disconnected from others, impulsively seeking short-term dopamine to numb themselves from the pain of the moment. The loss of purpose led to the death of the body.

Without meaning in their suffering or hope to move forward, happiness was impossible. In the absence of purpose, the present experience became a prison to be escaped either by thoughts of the past, suicide, or another form of deterioration.

Without a *why* to live for, every ounce of remaining life was used to escape the pain of the moment until they gasped for death like a drowning person gasps for air.

In *Man's Search for Meaning*, Frankl wrote:

> The prisoner who had lost faith in the future—his future—was doomed. With his loss of belief in the future, he also lost his spiritual hold; he let himself decline and became subject to mental and physical decay . . .
>
> Those who know how close the connection is between the state of mind of a man—his courage and hope, or lack of them—and the state of immunity of his body will understand that the sudden loss of hope and courage can have a deadly effect . . .
>
> Any attempt at fighting the camp's [pathological] influence on the prisoner by [therapeutic] methods had to aim at giving him inner strength by pointing out to him a future goal to which he could

look forward. Instinctively some of the prisoners attempted to find one on their own. It is a peculiarity of man that he can only live by looking to the future-*sub specie aeternitatis*. And this is his salvation in the most difficult moments of his existence.[5]

Frankl's use of the statement, *"sub specie aeternitatis,"* is important. It's an expression describing what is "universally and eternally true."

Frankl, of all people, would not use that term lightly.

This became the core tenet of Frankl's logotherapy: human beings are driven by their views of their own future. Having developed his theory prior to his imprisonment, Frankl's experiences in the concentration camps only magnified and clarified this perspective.

While a lack of purpose shortens life, having purpose can prolong and sustain life far beyond seemingly natural life expectancy. In the 18th century, the average life expectancy in America was less than 40 years. Yet, most of America's founding fathers lived at least 20 years longer. Several, including Benjamin Franklin, Thomas Jefferson, and John Adams lived into their eighties. That would be like three friends living to age 110 today, when 75 is the current life expectancy. Purpose provides an unparalleled life-force, vibrancy, and zest.

Frankl's purpose was to survive the camps so he could rewrite and publish his book. He deeply wanted to be reunited with his wife and family. Those goals kept Frankl alive. His why enabled him to bear almost any how.

According to Dr. Roy Baumeister and Dr. Kathleen Vohs, preeminent psychologists on the psychology of meaning, "Present events draw meaning from their connection to future outcomes."[6] Any human action or experience loses

meaning when disconnected to future outcomes or consequences. Nothing exists in a vacuum.

Why go to school or take classes if there is no end result?

Why work out or challenge yourself if there is no diploma?

Why make an emotional connection with another person if there is no relationship?

Why do anything at all?

The present is meaningless unless connected to the
future. It is the future that dictates which decisions
you opt for.

This was the dilemma those in the concentration camps
had to grapple with. Without hope toward a future, the present became incomprehensible. Without a Future Self, life no
longer drew a person onward. They literally lost their minds.

Frankl stated:

> A man who let himself decline because he could
> not see any future goal found himself occupied with
> retrospective thoughts. Instead of taking the camp's
> difficulties as a test of their inner strength, they did
> not take their life seriously and despised it as some-
> thing of no consequence. They preferred to close
> their eyes and to live in the past. Life for such people
> became meaningless.

For Frankl, hope and purpose toward your future is
the essential foundation to a meaningful and functional
life. Without hope, people's psychology unravels and dis-
torts. Individualistic and socially distant, those without a
future stop finding ways to make life better. They become
pure victims of external circumstances with no agency over
their lives.

As the Proverb states, "Where there is no vision, the people perish."[7] This perishing is an internal disintegration where personality and physical health abruptly reduce to nothing. For Frankl, having a purpose wasn't some vague hope or optimism, *but a tangible and specific goal.* In fact, he used the word *goal* most often to describe having a "meaning to fulfill" in your future. His description of having a purpose, meaning, or goal to accomplish squares exactly with modern research on the subject of hope.

To the average person, hope may seem like mere wishing. But think for a minute what your life would be like without hope in the future. Without something specific to look and build toward, the present becomes utterly painful. In this frenetic nightmare, you feel there is no control or escape from a downward spiral. Without hope, motivation is impossible. You can't be motivated toward action or outcome with zero hope in its possibility.

Without hope, grit is impossible. According to Dr. Angela Duckworth, grit is passion and perseverance toward long-term goals. From her standpoint, hope is the powerpack that sustains you through the ups and downs of whatever you're pursuing.[8]

Researchers describe hope as the will and the way.[9] Hope is the will because conscious choosing is involved. You decide a specific end, which you feel is worthwhile and important to create, pursue, or realize. You believe you have agency, and that your decisions matter, and that you can influence the outcomes of your life.

Hope is the way because to have hope, you either see a way to realize your goal, or are flexible enough to create a way. When hope exists, there is always a way. Hope does not consider the odds.

Hope is:

1. a clear and **specific goal**

2. **agency thinking**. Belief you have control over what you do, that your actions matter, and you can impact the results in your life.[10]

3. **pathways thinking**. You see a path, have a path, or can create multiple paths from where you are now to your goal.

Hope is more powerful than optimism, which is a general sense that the future will be better.[11,12,13] Having a glimmer of hope is akin to having a deposit already banked and earning interest on your future purpose.

But there is a much higher bar of hope. This degree requires commitment. It requires agency. It requires action.

Like hope on steroids, this level is the will *and* the way.

Psychologists have found distinct differences between high-hope people and low-hope people.[14,15] The differences can be summed up by a quote from Dr. Charles Snyder, the world's leading expert and researcher on hope:

> High-hope people find multiple pathways to reach their goals and willingly try new approaches. Low-hope people, on the other hand, stick with one approach and do not try other avenues when stymied. Instead of using problem-focused thought, the low-hope people often use counterproductive avoidance and disengagement thinking. Reinforced in the short term by their avoidance thoughts, low-hope people continue their passivity. Unfortunately, they do not learn from past experiences. High-hope people, however, use information about not reaching their goals as diagnostic feedback to search for other feasible approaches.[16]

High hope people commit 100 percent to a specific result. While their goal is unwavering, they remain highly flexible in the process or path to achieve their pursuit.

Dr. Angela Duckworth distilled an explanation of human maturity. According to her research, people get grittier as they age. To be gritty, you've got to stick with something for a long time, overcoming setbacks and obstacles along the way. Someone who switches from goal to goal to goal cannot gain that vital grit. An athlete who switches from one sport to another isn't gritty. Grit is sticking to one thing for years or even decades.

The second aspect of grit and maturity is just as important. Maturity comes by committing to a specific long-term goal, and regularly switching out or upgrading pathways or systems to realize the overarching goal.

To be a high-hope person, you commit to the goal, not the process. You don't get stuck in your current way of doing and thinking. Patiently, persistently you adapt and find new and better ways to get where you want to go.

As Frankl knew, hope is rooted in a clear purpose for your future. A high-hope person, like Frankl himself, remains committed 100 percent to a pursuit, and 100 percent flexible around the path to achieve their goal.

In the absence of a clear purpose for your life, your critical thinking to find ways deteriorates into finding excuses. After all, without hope, nothing really matters anyway.

The first and most fundamental threat to your Future Self is not having hope in your future.

Without hope, the present loses meaning.

Without hope, you don't have clear goals or a sense of purpose for your life.

Without hope, there is no way.

Without hope, you decay.

A REACTIVE NARRATIVE ABOUT YOUR PAST STUNTS YOUR FUTURE

"Everyone has a plan until they get punched in the face."

—Mike Tyson

When I was 16 years old, my mom, two brothers, and I took a trip to visit a close friend, Michael Barker, in Sun Valley, Idaho. Halfway through the five-hour evening drive, my mom grew tired. As a new driver, I eagerly offered to take the wheel. My mom lay in the backseat and quickly fell asleep.

Within minutes, I encountered a construction site with flashing lights signaling me into the left lane. In the dark rain, barriers blocked construction on the right side of the road, and once the barriers ended, I returned to the right lane. Suddenly, the tires dropped a foot into dirt and rubble. At 60 miles per hour, I instinctively yanked the wheel to get back into the left lane. The car spun into the freeway median and flipped. My head crashed against the window and I was knocked unconscious.

When I woke, the car had landed on the opposite side of the freeway. I heard my brother, Jacob, crying in the backseat.

"Ben," Trevor yelled, "Mom's not in the car!"

When the car flipped, Mom had been thrown and ragdolled 50 feet across the pavement. No child should see their parent in such a brutal state. I had no words.

Mercifully, paramedics quickly arrived, and we were taken by ambulance to the nearest hospital while Mom was life-flighted to an intensive unit. We didn't know if she was alive.

While we waited for news in the hospital that night, a police officer came into our room. "Which one of you is Ben?"

As I rose, I noticed a pile of hair on the pillow where I had lain. Noticing my surprise, the officer explained my hair was falling out because I was in shock.

He took me aside. "Look, this experience could ruin your entire life. I don't know what is going to happen with your mom. But right now, you need to make a choice about how you're going to handle this."

He told me that the person who was supposed to work the night shift and check the construction zone had been a no-show. More than 150 yards of tumbled construction barriers should have been put back in place. "This wasn't your fault. You're not to blame."

He helped me take ownership of the situation for myself and my younger brothers who needed me.

According to renowned trauma expert Dr. Peter Levine, "Trauma is not what happens to us, but what we hold inside in the absence of an empathetic witness."[17]

This police officer was my empathetic witness. He helped me process the shock and pain. He allowed me to cry. He helped me be proactive in how I framed this experience.

Everyone has a plan until life punches them in the face. Whatever punches life gives to you, your past is just a story. Whatever story you choose for your past enormously impacts your present and your future.

When you frame the past negatively, your goals become reactive to and based on your past. Your goals become short term and avoidance-oriented, where you try escaping the pain of the present.

When reactive, life happens *to* you, rather than *for* you. When reactive, you feel the victim to what life has done to you.

Emotional health happens when you contain both a positive past and an exciting future. Having a positive past depends very little on what events actually occurred. What happened *to* you doesn't matter as much as what story you decide to tell yourself about what happened. What happened *to* you doesn't matter as much as what emotions you feel about what happened.

Your past is fundamentally a *meaning*. The story you create about past events dictates what your past means to your present and to your Future Self.

We get to choose what story we attach. Grief expert and psychiatrist Gordon Livingston, M.D., said, "The stories of our lives, far from being fixed narratives, are under constant revision."[18]

From a psychological standpoint, time is more holistic than sequential. We often think of time as the past that is behind us, the present that we're now living, and the future that is ahead. But psychologically, the past, present, and future exist together here and now. "The past," said American novelist William Faulkner, "is never dead. It's not even past."[19]

Despite the fact that our past narrative largely impacts our future goals and hopes, our present state is largely what determines those critical past narratives. As we age and mature, we naturally reconstruct memories with different perspectives. We can choose to intentionally reframe a memory in a positive mood, safe environment, and around trusted people.

As psychologist Brent Slife states in *Time and Psychological Explanation* (italics mine):

> We reinterpret or reconstruct our memory in light of what our mental set is in the present. In this sense, *it is more accurate to say the present causes*

*the meaning of the past, than it is to say that the past
causes the meaning of the present . . .* Our memories
are not "stored" and "objective" entities but living
parts of ourselves in the present. This is the reason
our present moods and future goals so affect our
memories.[20]

To have a bigger future, first have a better past.

You can reframe and reshape your past narrative over
and over. As you become more mature, you'll look on even
your hardest moments with awe and joy. You'll love those
moments for what they continue to teach you, and for the
meaning they've given your life.

Yes, life is hard. Pain is part of the process. Every single person—regardless of their socioeconomic status, race,
or any other factor—will experience enormous amounts
of emotional pain in their life. Disappointments. Dashed
dreams. Unrealized expectations. Something truly horren-
dous. Or the harsh words and criticism too easily uttered.
The trauma of our own mistakes.

How we handle pain and confusion largely dictates
who our Future Self becomes. If you allow the pain of life
to swallow you, then your primary goals become to numb
yourself through addictions and distractions because you're
unwilling to face and transform those emotions.

Funneled effectively, pain and hurt are incredibly powerful teachers. Your hardest moments can push you to truly
learn from life and commit to something much better.
Indeed, change often occurs when the pain of not changing becomes more unbearable than the pain of change.

It may take years, even decades, to reframe an experience.
Or the shift can happen in a heartbeat. The life-giving power

is within you. With deliberate practice, you can develop the skill of positively reframing any past experience into a gain. With practice, you can get better and quicker at converting pain into growth and purpose.

Your pain can fuel your purpose and lead you to help others. This is what psychologists call post-traumatic growth, and it occurs as people proactively face pain and choose to view it with gratitude and appreciation.[21] You have the power to choose the framing of any experience, and your narration of it, as a positive.

Can you feel genuinely glad you went through your hardest moments? Without those, you wouldn't know what you now know or be who you are. Strategic Coach co-founder Dan Sullivan and I wrote an entire book on this subject called *The Gap and the Gain*.[22] The gap is when you measure yourself or your experiences against what you ideally thought they should be.

When you go through something terrible, and you frame the experience in the gap, then life is happening *to* you, and you're the byproduct of your experiences. You're the powerless victim of what happened. The gap leads to unhealthy comparisons and a lack of learning from your experiences.

The gain happens when you transform every experience into personal growth. No matter what occurs, frame the experience as a gain. Proactively and consciously learn from your experiences, and become better, not bitter, as a result. When you go through something terrible, and you frame the experience in the gain, then life is happening *for* you. Rather than being the byproduct of your experiences, your experiences are the byproduct of your conscious choosing. You determine what your experiences mean.

You own your experiences; they don't own you. Rather than devaluing your experiences because they were painful, you increase their value by learning more and more from them. You also have gratitude for your experiences. In the gain about your past, your Future Self continually grows bigger and better as a result of every experience you have.

When you're in the gain, you are more informed than your former self. You have greater perspective, purpose, and empathy. Your Future Self is better equipped because of your past.

Following that horrific traffic accident, my mom lay in a coma for several weeks. Somehow, someway, she survived.

She wore a body cast for more than a year. Her hair was cut to remove glass from her scalp. The vertebrae in her back were permanently altered, and two decades later, she continues to experience intense pain.

While in a coma, my mom felt as though she'd died. She told God she wanted to return to her body so she could raise her three sons. When she regained consciousness, she carried a profound sense of purpose to be alive. The nurses who worked with her were continually stunned by her positive attitude. Despite continual and excruciating pain, my mom expressed gratitude to be alive.

For years, our family struggled to discuss the accident. Yet, my Mom chooses to frame the event as a positive that solidified her purpose in life. She appreciates life's little things, which most people take for granted. No matter who you are, your status, or where you've been, my mom will embrace you. She embodies extreme compassion and care for every person. Far from bitter about what happened, she's better.

Threat #2 is having a reactive narrative about your past, which limits your future.

Your past is a meaning.

Your past is a story.

How you frame that story will largely impact your Future Self.

BEING UNAWARE OF YOUR ENVIRONMENT CREATES A RANDOM EVOLUTION

"You're the average of the five people you spend the most time with."

–Jim Rohn

In a famous study, a group of researchers told 2nd and 3rd grade teachers they wanted to study the learning of their students over the course of the school year. At the beginning of the year, the teachers were privately told which students were gifted and which ones weren't based on IQ tests the researchers had given them.[23]

As expected, by the end of the school year, the gifted students showed extremely higher increases in learning and overall development than the non-gifted students.

However, the researchers hadn't actually given the students IQ tests at the beginning of the year. Instead, they randomized which students were considered gifted and which ones weren't simply to see if it would influence their results.

Unconsciously and unknowingly, the teachers treated the gifted students differently than the non-gifted students. They expected more of those students, and those expectations became a self-fulfilling prophecy.[24]

We don't like to admit this, but our performance and results are often based on the expectations of those around us. Psychologists call this *the Pygmalion effect*.[25] If you're around people who have low expectations for you, you'll fall to those standards. If you're around people with high expectations, you'll rise to those standards.

We are all driven by our goals. But how often are goals unconsciously fed to us by our environment? Is it any wonder that my brother-in-law, with seven dentists on his mother's side, became a dentist? Can we fault the woman surrounded by drugs as a child, who turns to drugs for respite from her pain?

The more mature you become, the more proactive and conscious are the goals you choose for yourself. The less mature you remain, the more reactive and unconscious are the goals you pursue.

Threat #3 is being unaware of the impact of your environment on your goals.

As the Wharton marketing professor Dr. Jonah Berger explains in his book *Invisible Influence*, "Just like atoms bouncing off each other, our social interactions are constantly shaping who we are and what we do."[26]

Interestingly, psychologists found that people prefer things, not because of internal reasons, but simply because they've been repeatedly exposed to them. This idea is known as the *mere-exposure effect*.[27,28,29] Your desires are often the result of simply being exposed to something. For instance, research shows that people who were frequently exposed to cigarette commercials reported a more positive attitude toward smoking.[30]

This is true of your peer group. The proximity effect predicts that you're more likely to be friends with the person who sits next to you in class than the person who sits two rows ahead.

The public speaker and author Zig Ziglar said, "Your input determines your outlook. Your outlook determines your output, and your output determines your future." Better inputs lead to better thinking and ultimately better outputs. Garbage in, garbage out.

Do you want better and bigger goals? A better Future Self? Then expose yourself to better perspectives and evolved people. Business strategist Charlie Jones stated, "You will be the same person in five years as you are today except for the people you meet and the books you read." By proactively changing your inputs of information, experiences, and people, you become aware of what you previously didn't know. You see what you previously didn't notice. You seek what you previously didn't want. You act in ways you previously didn't behave.

Mindfulness is the skill of becoming aware of your context, and how that context influences you.[31] What is the context you're in?

How is that context influencing you?

What goals are you currently pursuing?

What is the life you're presently living?

How did you choose your life?

Is your life the product of conscious choosing, or are you merely reacting to your environment? Are your surroundings governing you, or do you influence your environment? Performance psychologist Dr. Marshall Goldsmith explained in his book *Triggers*, "If we do not create and control our environment, our environment creates and controls us."[32]

We live in a social media world designed to subconsciously influence and direct people's behaviors, desires, identities, and interests. Cultivating awareness of the impact of your external environment on your internal goals allows you to be mindful of when you're triggered in a certain direction, and consciously choose to realign with your Future Self. As Viktor Frankl put it:

Between stimulus and response there is a space.
In that space is our power to choose our response.
In our response lies our growth and our freedom.[33]

Freedom comes from not being the direct reaction of your environment. Instead, be aware of your environment, and scan externally for different perspectives and options. Expose yourself to new and better ways of acting, being, seeing, and thinking. In every situation, regardless of what you've done in the past, there is always the possibility to do otherwise. There is always potential for conscious choosing.

Who is the person you want to become? Your answer to this question will, obviously, be influenced by your current context. However, your answer should also extend beyond your current context. Imagination is more important than knowledge.

Who do you want to become, irrespective of your current situation and irrespective of your past? Rather than having goals that are reactive to your current context, it is far more powerful to mentally create the context you want, which is way beyond your current context, and use your future vision to drive your actions. As Harvard psychologist Dr. Ellen Langer said:

Social psychologists argue that who we are at any one time depends mostly on the context in which we find ourselves. But who creates the context? The more mindful we are, the more we can create the contexts we are in. When we create the context, we are more likely to be authentic. Mindfulness lets us see things in a new light and believe in the possibility of change.[34]

Once you've proactively begun imagining a Future Self beyond your current context, shape your environment to pull you in that direction. Instinctively, your brain will already and immediately begin doing this. As the Eastern mystic Rumi said, "What you seek is seeking you."

Once you decide upon something you want, your mind will become more aware of it in your environment. According to *selective attention*, you'll see things that were already all around, which you were previously blind to.[35,36] This awareness equips you to strategically find pathways and processes to get to where you want to go.

You'll be able to design your environment to become who you want to be. For instance, if you want to become an entrepreneur, surround yourself with successful entrepreneurs, not aspiring ones. To become healthy, surround yourself with people who are fit. If you want to be wealthy, go where abundance is the norm. Become the average of the people you surround yourself with.

Even Dr. Angela Duckworth, whose research focuses on grit—a fairly individualistic attribute—concedes that grit is much easier to develop and utilize in environments where high performance is the expected norm.[37] Becoming your desired Future Self involves aligning yourself with people who can help you get there.

The mere-exposure effect plus the Pygmalion effect.

Humans adapt amazingly quickly. Who you align yourself with has massive repercussions. If you hang out with people who play video games and eat junk food, you'll quickly grow to like and even love those behaviors. Conversely, spend time around active and productive people, you quickly take on those traits. A true friend makes your Future Self bigger.

As you align yourself personally and professionally with others, those relationships take you down a certain path. While some relationships are lifelong, most relationships are contextual. For instance, you may have a mentor or business partner who helps you for a period of time. But at a certain point, you may outgrow the relationship, and need to find a new teacher or partner.

What got you here won't get you there. It takes awareness, but also courage. It can be hard or scary to un-align with people you've been deeply connected with. But it can also be simple and respectful. Un-aligning doesn't mean someone is wrong or bad. Frequently your vision has evolved, and that relationship is no longer taking you in a shared direction.

To align yourself with specific people, you'll want to be *transformational* and not *transactional* in your mindset.

This doesn't mean that transactions or economics won't take place. They usually will. Additionally, this doesn't mean you're not strategic. Even the person you marry ought to be based on far more than mere infatuation. Instead, marry based on shared vision and purpose for your futures.

In transformational relationships, there is no keeping score. There's a genuine desire to help and support each other. The purpose and approach of the relationship is transformation, which focuses on giving, gratitude, and growth.

Rather than obsessing on "what's in it for me?" you ask, "what's in it for them?" You start the relationship by helping the other person better achieve their own goals.

Transformational relationships can take you places you never expected to go. Your Future Self can become unpredictably better and bigger. Transactional relationships can only take you so far. Your Future Self becomes greatly limited.

Threat #3 is that your Future Self is the byproduct of your environment. Being mindful enables your environment to be the result of your conscious choosing.

Choose well.

BEING DISCONNECTED FROM YOUR FUTURE SELF LEADS TO MYOPIC DECISIONS

when you're not connected to your future self
you make stupid decisions in the present

"The idea of long-term planning is a relatively new concept from a human evolution standpoint. We weren't evolved to live this long and have to make plans for the very distant future. Storing food for the next month or two, sure. But, to think about stocking away a retirement nest egg in case I'm retired for 30 years? This is relatively foreign. You couple that novel aspect of planning with the idea that we're very swayed by everything that is happening in the present. It's very easy to ignore the long, long run, and really hard to ignore all the pulls on our attention right now. Spending more money right now and eating something delicious right now—it's appealing to do those things because we know we get the rewards right now. But to not do those things—to not spend, to not eat unhealthily—so that our long-run selves can be better off, well, that's a hard proposition for a lot of people because the present is so powerful."

—Dr. Hal Hershfield[38]

As a species, we haven't evolved to plan 20 years into the future. As a rule, our decision-making is myopic, short-sighted, and lacks imagination. We're heavily incentivized to seek rewards in the present, which can greatly cost our long-term Future Selves.

According to Dr. Hal Hershfield, a UCLA psychologist who has invested 15 years studying the Future Self concept, the first step to farsighted decision-making is being connected to your Future Self. Connection starts with having empathy for your Future Self, just as you'd have empathy for another person.[39] To have empathy, you consider the other person's perspectives. You try to understand where *they* are coming from, and what matters *to them*.

Importantly, building a connection to your Future Self requires seeing your Future Self as a *different person* from who you are today.

This does not come naturally. As a rule, most people assume their Future Self is basically the same person they are today (see Truth #2).

By seeing your Future Self as a different person, you appreciate that this person sees things differently than you do now. They care about different things than you do now. They'd act differently than you would now.

Another step of empathy is appreciating how your actions, or inactions, impact the other person. In this case, how are your current behaviors impacting your Future Self? The more conscious you become of how everything you do right now impacts the person you are in the future, the better and more thoughtful your actions will be.

Hershfield found a direct correlation between the level of connection you have with your Future Self and the quality of your decisions right now. Beyond empathy, building a deep connection is truly liking the other person. You see the other person as your friend, someone you care about who genuinely cares for you.[40]

When you truly care about another person, you aren't put-off by making sacrifices of your time, energy, and resources for them. You'll sacrifice spending money now so your Future Self can have more money later. You'll sacrifice momentary gratifications to invest in education, health, and relationships.

Moving from liking to loving your Future Self is the difference between sacrificing for someone and investing. When I truly care about something or someone, I happily invest in that thing or relationship.

If I care about piano, I'll invest more to learn to play.

If I care about someone, I'll invest in the growth of that relationship.

If I care about me, I invest in myself so I can continually upgrade my thinking, opportunities, and skills. When I care about my Future Self, I happily invest in their well-being, situation, freedoms, and characteristics.

I happily make these investments. I want to make these investments, because I know that every time I invest in my Future Self, my life gets better.

As you invest in your Future Self, you are more connected to them.

You love whatever you invest yourself in.

You become committed to whatever you invest yourself in.

Over time, whatever you invest in grows and compounds.

Investing in your Future Self brings you closer to that person you are growing into. As you love them more, your Future Self expands exponentially. As your vision of your Future Self grows, your present happiness and motivation increases. Dan Sullivan said, "The only way to make your present better is by making your future bigger."

A clear and obvious threat to your Future Self is not being connected to them. Hershfield found that most people don't spend much time thinking about their Future Self. Caught up in the short-term dopamine of the present, like randomly scrolling through social media, binge eating, or binge spending, seeking short-term rewards creates long-term costs. When you engage in short-term reward seeking that produces negative long-term consequences, then you're costing your Future Self.

Whenever you engage in long-term reward behaviors where the benefits continue long into the future, you're investing in your Future Self.

Everything you do is either a cost to or an investment in your Future Self. Costs put your Future Self deeper in debt. Investments make your Future Self wealthier.

Do you want your Future Self to be broke and unhealthy, or fit and free?

The more you engage in short-term reward seeking, the fuzzier your long-term Future Self will become. You won't be able to envision beyond the next few days, weeks, or maybe months.

The more you invest in long-term rewards, the clearer your Future Self becomes. This creates what Hershfield calls vividness, an extremely advanced form of connection with your Future Self. The more vivid and detailed your Future Self, the more direct can be your process to get there.

A vivid future is a compelling future. Practiced at investing in your Future Self and achieving small milestones along the way, you'll envision in extreme detail your Future Self as a person, your environment, context, and daily life.

Hershfield found that it's actually easier to bring your Future Self to you than to go to your Future Self. Make your

Future Self vivid and detailed by writing a letter *from* your Future Self to your current self. Choose whatever time frame you want.

For example, put yourself in the shoes of your Future Self five years from now. Imagine what their life is like, and then write a letter, as your Future Self, talking to the current you. Have your Future Self describe what their life is like.

Don't get complicated.

Don't overthink.

Take as long or as little as you want on this, 5 minutes or 60. Have the flexibility and imagination to just write.

As you practice imagining your Future Self, you get better and clearer at being connected with them. If in the beginning it feels a little awkward or difficult, then just write in broad generalities. But also, be playful. This is simply a conversation between your Future Self and you. No one else is here. No one else is looking. Have fun.

Through this exercise, I've been able to see the exact house where my Future Self will live. I can see how my Future Self spends time, how much money they make, and how happy they feel. The more I invest in my Future Self, the more we collaborate together to create a profoundly powerful life.

For additional help connecting with your Future Self, visit futureself.com. There you can write a letter from your Future Self to make them more vivid.

The 4th Threat to your Future Self is not being connected to them. You will not be able to proactively create the life you want if you're not connected to your Future Self.

You won't be able to think and strategize long term.

You'll be caught up by endless distractions throughout your day.

Your decisions will be myopic.

You'll cost your Future Self greatly, putting them deeper in debt in all ways.

THREAT #5

URGENT BATTLES AND SMALL GOALS KEEP YOU STUCK

"*By our nature as rational, conscious creatures, we cannot help but think of the future. But most people, out of fear, limit their view of the future to a narrow range. Thoughts of tomorrow, a few weeks ahead, perhaps a vague plan for the months to come. We are generally dealing with so many immediate battles that it is hard for us to lift our gaze above the moment. It is a law of power, however, that the further and deeper we contemplate the future, the greater our capacity to shape it to our desires.*"

−50 Cent and Robert Greene, *The 50th Law*[41]

In the 2011 science fiction film *In Time,* Justin Timberlake portrays a character named Will Salas, who lives in the ghetto. Instead of money, *time* is the only currency, and everyone has a digital clock embedded into their arm indicating the amount of time they have. For example, rather than a cup of coffee costing $4 dollars, it costs four minutes. There are small devices used in this society, similar to a credit card machine, that add or take away time when scanned on a person's arm clock.

Until the age of 25, your clock doesn't start ticking. Once you hit your 25th birthday, you have one year's time on your clock, which immediately starts ticking down. After age 25, you stop physically aging. Whether you're 28, 49, or 302, you look as you did when your clock started ticking. You live as long as you have time.

The people living in the ghetto are living day-to-day, while those in the highest Time Zone can conceivably live forever with decades or centuries of time on their clocks. In the ghetto, people depend on the time added to their clocks at the end of each work shift. They get just enough time to get them to the end of tomorrow's shift where they'll get their next allotment.

Chained to their jobs or other dangerous and desperate means for their livelihood, those in the ghetto rarely have more than 24 hours on their clocks. They don't have enough time to step away from their rat race to strategize or think about creating a better future.

A fundamental aspect of the film is that, once you clock out or run out of time, you die. People in the ghetto are found dead on the streets all the time. There's a day-to-day mad rush and desperation to survive. There is no thriving.

In the film, economic status is portrayed as a higher Time Zone with better jobs and living conditions.

- To get out of the ghetto and into the lower-middle-class Time Zone costs *one months'* time

- To get from the lower-middle-class Time Zone into the middle class costs *two months' time*

- To get from the middle-class Time Zone into the upper middle class costs *six months' time*

- To get from the upper-middle-class Time Zone into New Greenwich, which represents the one percent of the one percent mega-wealthy costs *one year's worth of time*

The cost of living in each Time Zone also goes up dramatically. The restaurants in New Greenwich charge more than a month of time for a meal. The houses cost several years or decades. Crossing to a higher Time Zone requires the income to support that higher lifestyle.

The probability of someone in the ghetto ever accumulating a month of time is unlikely. And the people who newly turn 25 rarely go to the higher Time Zones because to do so, they'd have to leave family behind. Will's family was in such deep debt that all of his time was spent and gone a week after his 25th birthday.

An interesting thing to note is that everything feels slower in the higher Time Zones. Because people have an enormous amount of time, they are never in a rush. Conversely, the people in the lower Time Zones have far less time, so they're always rushing and busy. It's much more stressful.

Similar to that sci-fi movie, most human behavior is driven by very short-term goals including eating, paying bills, getting to work, getting the kids to school, rotating the tires, and brushing your teeth. It's day-to-day living, or at most, month-to-month living with an occasional vacation planned in there.

In 1906, Alfred Henry Lewis stated, "There are only nine meals between mankind and anarchy." Many people are around nine meals away from hunger. Most don't have a 6-month food supply. They don't have 12 months of emergency cash.

The reason they're living day-to-day is because their goals are day-to-day. Get to work. Get to lunch. Get to the end of the day. Get to the weekend. Pay the bills. The future many pursue is only a step ahead and we feel like the system is designed to keep people stuck in this survival-mode way of living.

If you're living day-to-day, you're always in a hurry.

When you're engaged in short-term goals, your time spirals quicker and quicker. Like a hamster on a wheel, you're living lots of years and expending lots of energy, but not making progress.

To exit the rat race of day-to-day mindset requires a shift in your focus. Connect to a bigger future. If you get serious, and started investing and learning, *where could you be in five years?*

In five years, MrBeast went from a 17-year-old kid with no money and little skills to making tens of millions of dollars, and being one of the most famous people in the world.

The way to slow time down and really make progress is to lift your gaze and begin thinking much bigger and further out. The 34th United States president, Dwight D. Eisenhower, famously said, "I have two kinds of problems: the urgent and the important. The urgent are not important, and the important are never urgent."

Business strategist Dr. Stephen Covey used rocks, pebbles, and a bucket to teach time management. In the activity, he filled the bucket with the small pebbles and then added the medium and large rocks. However, with the small pebbles taking up the bottom half of the bucket, the medium and large rocks couldn't all fit.

He emptied the bucket and started over, this time putting in the medium and large rocks first, and pouring the pebbles into the gaps around the larger rocks. By "putting first things first," like magic, everything else fits in the same space. Putting the pebbles in first is majoring in minor things.

Covey said the bucket symbolizes our time. The medium and large rocks represent important activities such as relationships, planning, learning, and health. The pebbles represent urgent activities such as checking email and going to meetings.

When we put the urgent before the important, we never get to the important. Playwright Meredith Willson wrote, "You pile up enough tomorrows, and you'll find you are left with nothing but a lot of empty yesterdays."

The only way off the day-to-day hamster wheel is to *prioritize* the important. You give yourself space to think beyond your current context, and really start investing in yourself. Put the important before the urgent.

Lift your gaze and begin connecting with your longer term Future Self.

Develop goals that are five years out, and prioritize those big goals *before* the urgent daily battles.

Threat #5 is thinking far too short term and urgent in your goals, and way too small about your future. This is a formula to exhaust extreme effort but stay in the same place.

After grinding away the first 50 years of his life, business mogul Grant Cardone realized that while his work ethic was solid, his goals were too small. You can work 80 hours per week toward a six-figure income or you can work 80 hours per week toward a seven- or eight-figure income. The amount of work isn't what really matters. It's what that work is going toward. As Cardone explains in his book *The 10X Rule*:

> Personally, the biggest mistake I've made is failing to set my targets high enough—in both personal and professional aspects of my life. It takes the same amount of energy to have a great marriage as it does an average one, just as it takes the same amount of energy and effort to make $10 million as it does $10,000.[42]

Grant Cardone was born March 28, 1959, in Lake Charles, Louisiana. He published *The 10X Rule* in 2011 when he was

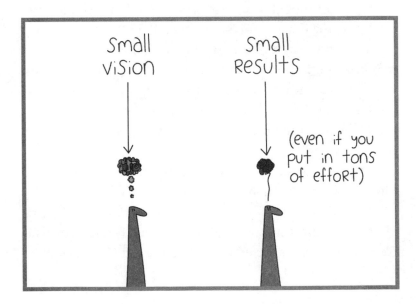

52 years old. The release of that book was an inflection point in Cardone's career. A relatively successful millionaire, he ran sales and real estate companies since the late 1980s.

But when he published *The 10X Rule* and committed to living a much higher vision, he became far more courageous and bolder. In 2012, he made the single largest private equity acquisition in Florida, consisting of five large-scale properties. From 2011 to 2021, he 10X'd his net worth from approximately $20 million to more than $300 million, creating a portfolio worth several billion dollars. Cardone radically elevated his vision.

What opportunities are you missing simply because you're so focused on your urgent and small goals?[43,44] Suffering from *inattentional blindness*, people are so busy looking for bronze coins that they *can't see* the gold coins all around them.

You get what you're looking for. You see what you're currently measuring. All the while, there are insane, life-changing opportunities sitting in front of your face *right now*. Gold coins.

The problem for you and me is we don't see these opportunities. To see the world differently, ask different questions.

Rather than ask, "How can I make $100,000 this year?" ask, "How can I make $10,000,000 this year?"

Different questions spark innovative thinking and new angles. Psychologist and spiritual teacher Dr. Wayne Dyer said, "When you change the way you see things, the things you see change."[45] When you change what you're looking for, you change what you see.

Trade inattentional blindness for selective attention. Clarify what you're looking for, and you'll see it everywhere.

What was once hidden in plain sight will become radically obvious. You see what you're looking for.

Make your vision absurdly bigger and you'll immediately see pathways to get there. Dan Sullivan said, "Our eyes only see and our ears only hear what our brain is looking for."

A massive threat to your Future Self is simply that you're thinking way too small. Multiply your vision 10-times or 100-times larger. You'll be forced to understand the principles, rules, and strategies of living at a higher level. Instead of working harder, elevate what you think you can do. As the late advertising legend Paul Arden said:

> You need to aim beyond what you are capable of. You need to develop a complete disregard for where your abilities end. If you think you're unable to work for the best company in its sphere, make that your aim. If you think you're unable to be on the cover of Time magazine, make it your business to be there. Make your vision of where you want to be a reality. Nothing is impossible.[46]

A pervasive threat to your Future Self is being caught up in both urgent and small goals.

THREAT #6

NOT BEING IN THE ARENA IS FAILING BY DEFAULT

"It is not the critic who counts; not the man who points out how the strong man stumbles, or where the doer of deeds could have done them better. The credit belongs to the man who is actually in the arena, whose face is marred by dust and sweat and blood; who strives valiantly; who errs, who comes short again and again, because there is no effort without error and shortcoming; but who does actually strive to do the deeds; who knows great enthusiasms, the great devotions; who spends himself in a worthy cause; who at the best knows in the end the triumph of high achievement, and who at the worst, if he fails, at least fails while daring greatly, so that his place shall never be with those cold and timid souls who neither know victory nor defeat."

—Theodore Roosevelt

Tom Brady, the NFL quarterback, is widely considered the GOAT (greatest of all time) of football, and maybe even team sports in general. He has seven Superbowl victories and holds many other records. But perhaps, what is most amazing about Tom is his longevity. At the writing of this book, he is 44 years old.

Physically average, Tom was never the most athletic player. In fact, he's pretty slow and uncoordinated. He was selected as the 199th pick in the sixth round of the 2000 NFL draft. There appeared to be nothing remarkable about him and throughout his career, people doubted Tom.

"He'll never be a great quarterback."

"He's not athletic."

Even after he proved his doubters wrong by winning on the field, as he got older, the doubters continued. "He's too old to play."

In an episode of Tom's recent ESPN documentary, *Man in the Arena*, Tom talked about how the doubters and skeptics throughout his career aren't actually in the arena. Nothing they say or do has any impact on what occurs on the field.

Bo Eason, the former NFL player, said that when he watches sports on TV, he mutes the sound unless the commentator was an actual player. "Sports on TV are made for fans, not for pros. Pros don't watch that stuff. It's not made for them. It's made for spectators."

Interestingly, in America, sports commentary is nearly as popular, if not more popular, than the sports themselves. In these commentaries, people in the stands criticize and critique those in the arena. Armchair quarterbacking has become a prestigious and impressive pastime.

People muttering in their suits and waxing eloquent from the sidelines.

No matter what you do, there will be bystanders outside the arena who criticize. They will doubt you. They may even try protecting you from the rigors and dangers of the arena.

The former publisher of *SUCCESS* magazine, Darren Hardy, said, "Never take advice from someone you wouldn't trade places with."[47] Whenever you seek mentorship, only do so with people who are in the arena. Get advice from people who have experience with the battles you face.

Although the opinions of those outside the arena can be a distraction, the much bigger threat your Future Self faces is you staying out of the arena entirely, or for far too long.

Being outside the arena means you're overthinking, caught in paralysis by analysis. You're letting fear win. Take for example, the countless people who want to start a business, or write a book, or learn a language, or [fill in the blank] of any dream someone might have.

The philosopher Cato said, "He who hesitates is lost." The longer you hesitate to enter the playing field, the longer you delay the essential learning curve. You cannot deliberately practice on the sidelines. When you're not in the arena, you're failing by default.

Outside the arena may feel safe, but it's the most dangerous place you could be. While outside, you remain ignorant of your own ignorance. You may be an armchair philosopher on whatever subject you're interested in, but you're not becoming a pro. Staying on the sidelines leads to a life of regrets.

The psychological definition of courage is to proactively pursue a noble and worthwhile goal involving risk.[48,49] According to Dr. David Hawkins, courage is the doorway to all positive change.[50] It takes courage to get into the game because once in the arena, *you will fail.* You'll immediately get hit in the face with the consequences of your actions and your ignorance. And although painful in the moment, this is exactly how you learn and adapt.

When you were outside the arena, you may not have felt like you were failing. But every day you sit on the sidelines, you fail by default. It took me five years to convince myself to start writing online. I'd gotten home from my church mission in 2010 and knew I wanted to be a writer. But it wasn't until 2015 that I finally entered the arena and began learning and making progress.

Once I put my work out there, I got some support. But I also received pretty rough feedback and criticism. As my work got more popular, the criticism got worse. Harder than dealing with the criticism of those outside the arena, I had to face my own insecurities. Sharing my ideas, thoughts, and emotions publicly? Learning how to do it well? Learning how to write effectively, and under a deadline?

It was tough. But I was in the arena. I was learning fast. Every step I took deeper into the arena, the more I saw things my former self had been completely blind to. I learned how to grow a business, and connect with the right mentors and influencers. I developed collaborations that led to publishing deals and other incredible opportunities.

But the actions and behaviors at mile marker "E" were completely blind to me at mile marker "C." I had to actually get in the arena to understand the landscape. My failures were my best friend. I learned from others in the arena who were steps ahead of me.

The same thing occurred when Lauren and I became foster parents to our three kids. You could read hundreds of books on a subject, but those books pale to the tangible experience of doing. Information becomes useful when you're in the arena because you need real solutions, and you need them right now. The consequences for failure are very real in the arena.

When you're on the sidelines, you can enjoy theorizing and armchair quarterbacking. There are no real risks or consequences. Once you're in the arena, and dealing with the realities of the situation, then you can engage in applied learning where you get filtered information you can use right now. As a new foster parent, I remember the sleepless nights, dealing with our children's emotional challenges. Who could blame them? They'd been taken away from their parents and were living with strangers. Every day, it felt like I was failing. Seven years later, I can still feel like all I'm doing is failing as a father.

But I'm in the arena.

I'm learning.

I know way more about parenting than I did seven years ago, or seven days ago. And I'm comfortable failing or learning. I'm fine making mistakes because the mistakes I make now are much more important than the mistakes I made a few years ago. I'm playing a much bigger game than I was a few years ago. The stakes are a lot higher. The love is deeper. Every victory is more rewarding.

When you're not in the arena, you can enjoy the fantasy football equivalent of whatever you're dreaming about, but you get few genuine rewards. You're more ignorant than you realize.

Spectators are caught in paralysis by analysis, fear, and decision fatigue. The longer you wait to enter your arena, the more you limit your Future Self.

Being in the arena means you're finally facing and embracing *reality*. In the arena, you're no longer afraid of reality because it has become your instructor. Eventually, as your Future Self you'll be able to shape reality.

SUCCESS IS OFTEN THE CATALYST FOR FAILURE

"The second-richest man in America, Warren Buffett, says one of his biggest challenges is to help his top people—all wealthy beyond belief—stay interested enough to jump out of bed in the morning and work with all the enthusiasm they did when they were poor and just getting started . . . Success Disease makes people begin to forego to different degrees the effort, focus, discipline, teaching, teamwork, learning, and attention to detail that brought 'mastery' and its progeny, success."

—Bill Walsh[51]

The Beatles changed music forever in a relatively brief time span, bursting onto the scene in 1963 with *Please Please Me,* and recording their last albums, *Let It Be* and *Abbey Road*, in 1969.

Why did the most influential band of the 20th century break up within seven years of releasing their first album? The band was a phenomenal success. They become global icons. They made millions and millions of dollars.

With success comes increased complexity.

When the Beatles started out together, they were buddies writing and playing songs. They had a singular focus and aligned goals. But as they become successful, their situation and goals became more complex and less united. Divisions grew within the group.

Increasing external parties had voice and say in what the Beatles should be doing. Lennon and McCartney couldn't see eye-to-eye about how to manage the group, especially after their band manager, Brian Epstein, died in 1967. Despite being arguably the best band of all time, their own success, and all that came with success, eventually led to the death of the Beatles.

The seventh and final threat to your Future Self is, interestingly, success.

The Beatles are one of countless examples of this phenomenon dubbed *success disease*, or "when success eats itself."

Success is difficult to handle. Most people self-destruct once things start getting good. Dr. Gay Hendricks developed a concept he calls "the upper limit problem," which he uses to explain how success can backfire. From Hendricks's perspective, we all have a subconscious baseline of where we're comfortable, and when we succeed in some area of our lives, we subconsciously self-sabotage back to our baseline. He describes:

> Each of us has an inner thermostat setting that determines how much love, success, and creativity we allow ourselves to enjoy. When we exceed our inner thermostat setting, we will often do something to sabotage ourselves, causing us to drop back into the old, familiar zone where we feel secure.[52]

If you've never had a lot of money and you start making good money, you may subconsciously do something stupid to flush all that new money down the drain.

Becoming successful in whatever arena you choose requires a great deal of clarity, focus, and a longer-term commitment to your Future Self. By continually investing and deliberately practicing toward your Future Self, you can become highly successful. You can create dreams far beyond your initial conception.

However, with growing success comes growing complexity. In the beginning, you were just focused on your passion or craft. But then, so many other opportunities far beyond the life of your former self enter the equation such as managing money, time, and key relationships. Each decision must be filtered quickly to avoid paralysis by analysis.

As your focus and long-term vision are squeezed out by short-term wins, the original singular goal becomes muddled and distracted. Flow and focus drown if you can't manage and filter complexity. What truly matters becomes harder to discern as you work harder but no longer make the massive progress you once knew. As time and attention spread thin, this lack of clarity and focus inevitably leads to downfall.

As author Greg McKeown explains:

Why don't successful people and organizations automatically become very successful? One important explanation is due to what I call "the clarity paradox," which can be summed up in four predictable phases:

- Phase 1: When we really have clarity of purpose, it leads to success.

- Phase 2: When we have success, it leads to more options and opportunities.

- Phase 3: When we have increased options and opportunities, it leads to diffused efforts.

- Phase 4: Diffused efforts undermine the very clarity that led to our success in the first place.

Curiously, and overstating the point in order to make it, success is a catalyst for failure.[53]

Author and philosopher Robert Brault said, "We are kept from our goal not by obstacles, but by a clear path to a lesser goal."[54] The more successful you become, the more lesser goals present themselves. The more opportunities and quick wins come your way, the greater the need to continually update your vision to filter out the 99 percent of nonessential traps to your energy and focus.

Becoming successful at what you do is far less difficult than maintaining and expanding that success. In the field of sports, teams that reach the top rarely repeat as champions. Complacent because they've achieved their goal, their focus shifts. Success brings opportunity and distraction, and players stop putting in the focused work and deliberate practice needed to be at the top.

When things are going well, it's also easy to get soft and lazy. You stop the disciplines that got you where you're at. In the novel *Those Who Remain: A Postapocalyptic Novel*, author G. Michael Hopf wrote:

> Hard times create strong men. Strong men create good times. Good times create weak men. And, weak men create hard times.[55]

As times get good, people become less focused and less committed. They stop having a bigger Future Self they're driving toward. They get stuck in short-term dopamine loops. Their actions and behaviors lead to unnecessary bad times. The law of the harvest. You reap what you sow.

On a global scale, every great nation or empire that has ever existed eventually fell. Success led to failure. Famed historians Will and Ariel Durant summarized the rise and fall of nations in the book *The Lessons of History*.[56] Human civilization has gone through three core stages:

1. Hunting

2. Agriculture

3. Industry

The hunting stage focused on the individual. Brutal, barbaric, and extremely competitive, each individual focused on themselves.

The agricultural stage focused on family. Children were raised to work on the farm. People married early and had kids early to help with the needed work. Divorce was rare. Although competitive, there was more collaboration as farmers traded and bartered with other farmers.

The industrial stage is focused on the group. As technology and society grows, people leave the farm to live in the city. Marriage becomes less important. People have fewer children. Government, education, and technology replace religion.

Yet, according to the Durants, this is where the downfall begins. From their perspective, to thrive in a societal group, individual members must obey a moral code that supports the group interests over individual interests. This can be difficult for people whose individualistic evolution runs deep. Without religion to provide meaning for living a moral code, people have less reason to do what's best for the group. With the loss of religion, communism eventually rises, diminishing freedom and progress.

Communism fails, according to the Durants, because inequality between humans is a fundamental aspect of nature and society. Communism seeks to force equality, and thus destroys freedom and autonomy.

When you take away freedoms, and when people are no longer choosing of their own free will to support the betterment of society, then that society crumbles.

The Durants explain:

> Heaven and utopia are buckets in a well: when one goes down the other goes up; when religion declines Communism grows."

The Durants believe that America, the world's current superpower, will eventually crumble for the same reasons previous empires failed.

Ray Dalio, the American billionaire and hedge fund manager, has a slightly more nuanced perspective. In Dalio's book *Principles for Dealing with the Changing World Order: Why Nations Succeed and Fail*, he lays out the core reasons a society fails.[57] Just like a business, when a nation takes on extreme levels of debt, becomes less productive, and is riddled with internal division, it is poised for a collapse.

Despite still being incredibly strong, Dalio sees America checking many of the wrong boxes.

Success can be hard to handle for individuals, teams, organizations, and nations. Becoming successful is one thing, but expanding that success is something entirely different. You may even get lax as things start getting good.

Why should this matter to you?

If you get clear on your Future Self, and invest specifically toward your Future Self, you will become incredibly successful. You'll experience the compound effect in knowledge, skills, money, and relationships. But with this increase in success, you will face surprising complexity.

To guard against collapse requires clarifying your Future Self at each succeeding stage. Success breeds a barrage of distractions and lesser goals. Without remaining clear on what truly matters, you'll become internally divided on what you're committed to. As the Bible states, "A double minded man is unstable in all his ways."[58]

Success is a massive threat to your Future Self.

CONCLUSION

FUTURE SELF THREATS

Your Future Self is not set in stone.

There are an infinite number of directions your life can go.

Your Future Self is inevitable.

In 2 years, 5 years, 10 years, or 20, baring fatality, you will become someone. The question to ask yourself is: Who will your Future Self be? That is, perhaps, the most important question any human can ask themself.

In this section of the book, we've covered the seven core threats to your Future Self. These threats, if unchecked, will lead to your Future Self being someone far less than your potential.

Next, we dive into the seven core truths about your Future Self. As you fully grasp the truths of your Future Self, you'll be equipped to dictate who your Future Self becomes. You'll have the power to create a life beyond anything you currently imagine.

Truth #1:   Your future drives your present

Truth #2:   Your Future Self is different than you expect

Truth #3:   Your Future Self is the Pied Piper

Truth #4:   The more vivid and detailed your Future Self, the faster you'll progress

Truth #5:   Failing as your Future Self is better than succeeding as your current self

Truth #6:   Success is achieved by being true to your Future Self, nothing else

Truth #7:   Your view of God impacts your Future Self

(PART 2)

7 TRUTHS ABOUT YOUR FUTURE SELF

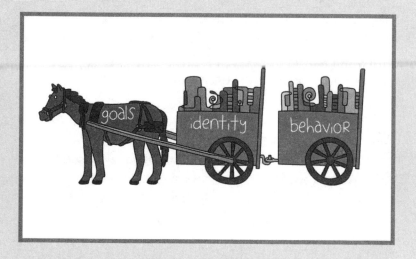

"What man actually needs is not a tensionless state but rather the striving and struggling for a worthwhile goal, a freely chosen task. What he needs is not the discharge of tension at any cost but the call of a potential meaning waiting to be fulfilled by him."

—Viktor Frankl[1]

Ferdinand Marcos was a very good liar.

On December 30, 1965, he became the 10th president of the Philippines by claiming to be the "most decorated war hero in all of the Philippines."

Once president, Marcos pursued an aggressive program of infrastructure development throughout the Philippines, building new roads, schools, and other complexes funded by foreign debt. His extreme spending initially won him popularity.

During his second term, Marcos's spending and debt accumulation snowballed into an inflation crisis. The Philippine economy plummeted, and social unrest threatened.

Marcos didn't care that his people suffered. During his presidency, he and his family enjoyed a lavish lifestyle funded by money stollen from the Central Bank of the Philippines. *Guinness* awarded the Marcos family the world record for the largest-ever theft from a government: an estimated 5 to 10 billion dollars.[2]

As president, Marcos invested absurd amounts of money into his military, not to protect his people from foreign invaders, but to control and punish anyone who didn't follow his strict laws.

During Marcos's reign, the Philippines fell deeply in debt. Socially and morally corrupt, the nation was split by internal division and strife.

Many wanted to overthrow the government, including a young and rising politician named Benigno ("Ninoy") Aquino Jr. Born into a political family, Ninoy was elected mayor in 1955 when he was only 23 years old. Five years later, at age 27, he became the nation's youngest vice governor.

A family man, in 1954 he married Corazon ("Cory") Sumulong Cojuangco, a well-educated Catholic woman from an affluent Filipino family. During Ninoy's rising career, Cory primarily focused on raising their growing family of five children, supporting her husband's career, and offering great wisdom in his decision-making.

In 1968, during his first year as senator, Ninoy accused Marcos of corruption and establishing a garrison state by ballooning the armed forces budget. Ninoy boldly criticized the president and his wife, Imelda, for their extravagant lifestyles and fraud.

Ninoy's following grew and he became the leading candidate to replace Marcos as president in the 1971 elections. His why was strong. He envisioned a Philippines characterized by democracy and freedom, moral laws, good leadership, and a people united and abundant.

On August 21, 1971, there was a kickoff rally for the Liberal Party with crowds cheering and bands playing. Suddenly, two bombs exploded, killing 8 people and critically wounding 120 others. Ninoy was not present at the rally, despite being the Liberal candidate, and Marcos claimed Ninoy orchestrated the bombing.

This event sparked a chain of political and social unrest over the next year. Marcos used the growing chaos as an opportunity to further his aims. He was barred by the 1935 Constitution to seek a third presidential term, but on September 21, 1972, he declared martial law. Shortly thereafter, he abolished the existing constitution, allowing himself to remain in office.

Under martial law, Marcos immediately arrested Ninoy and sentenced him to death. Ninoy spent the next eight years in prison awaiting his trial. Isolated, Cory raised her five children alone.

After nearly six years in prison, Ninoy remained committed to the democracy of his country. He did a hunger strike, which nearly killed him, and in 1978 ran for president from his prison cell.

In mid-March 1980, Ninoy suffered a severe heart attack. He was transported from prison to the Philippine Heart Center, where he suffered a second heart attack. Despite ECG tests that showed a blocked artery, Philippine surgeons were reluctant to perform the coronary bypass. No one wanted to give Marcos a reason to retaliate.

Fearing tampering by Marcos, Ninoy refused to have Philippine doctors treat him. His request to travel to the United States with his family for the surgery was granted, conditional that he immediately return once healthy and say absolutely nothing negative about Marcos while abroad.

Ninoy recovered quickly and renounced the agreement he made with Marcos, saying, "a pact with the devil is no pact at all." During the next three years—from 1980 to 1983—Ninoy, Cory, and their children lived in Boston. To support his family, Ninoy wrote two books and lectured nationwide while living on fellowship grants from Harvard University.

In early 1983, Ninoy learned of the deteriorating political situation back home, as well as of Marcos's failing health. He felt compelled to return and speak to Marcos about returning the country to democracy before extremists took over. Ninoy knew returning to the Philippines could cost him his life.

Martin Luther King, Jr. said, "If a man hasn't found something he will die for, he isn't fit to live."

International airlines were warned that they'd be denied landing rights and forced to return if they attempted to fly

Ninoy back to the Philippines. Barred from entering the Philippines, Ninoy secured a fake passport from a separatist group opposing Marcos. Through a series of precarious flights, Ninoy landed in the Philippines on August 21, 1983.

Sensing his own doom, he wore a bulletproof vest and told the journalists accompanying him on the flight:

> You have to be very ready with your hand camera because this action can become very fast. In a matter of a three or four minutes it could be all over, and [laughing] I may not be able to talk to you again after this.

Once the plane landed at Manila International Airport, Ninoy stepped out onto the staircase leading to the tarmac and was immediately shot in the head and killed. Ninoy's assassination was a tipping point for the nation, and galvanized a surge of opposition, protest, and discontent against the Marcos government.

Ten days after his death, on August 31, 1983, Ninoy's funeral mass was held at Santo Domingo Church in Santa Mesa Heights, Quezon City. Ninoy's mother, Aurora, told the funeral parlor not to make up or embalm his body, so everyone could see "what they did to my son." More than two million people lined the streets for the procession.

The jury acquitted all 26 defendants involved in the murder of Cory's husband. Despite staying out of the limelight, this was her moment of decision. In the words of the historian Will Durant, "The ability of the average [person] could be doubled, if the situation demanded it."[3]

Cory committed to overthrow the Marcos regime and restore democracy to the Philippines. The self-described housewife became the figurehead of the anti-Marcos movement.

In the lead-up to the 1986 presidential election, and sensing the growing momentum against him, Marcos suddenly announced snap elections. A petition quickly spread urging Cory to run for president. In response to the millions who signed the petition, Cory announced her candidacy on December 3, 1985.

During his campaign, Marcos viciously attacked Cory, saying she was "just a woman" who had no experience.

Cory responded calmly:

> I don't have experience in cheating, lying to the public, stealing government money, or killing political opponents. So, I do agree I have less political experience than the kind that you're talking about.

The snap election on February 7, 1986, was rigged in Marcos's favor. On February 15, Marcos claimed to be the winner and threatened those who supported Cory with violence and intimidation.

Cory and more than two million others gathered to protest through peaceful civil disobedience.

Global leaders throughout the world expressed their support for Cory, including the United States.

On February 22, several Filipino military generals announced their support for Cory, and stood against the Marcos government. They established operations at the Armed Forces of the Philippines headquarters. Millions of Filipinos gathered to support the rebel military and Cory flew to Manila to prepare to take over the presidency.

After three days of peaceful mass protests, called the Power People Revolution, Cory was sworn in as the 11th president of the Philippines on February 25, 1986. She became the first female president in all of Asia.

That same day, Marcos and his wife fled the Philippines for Hawaii by way of Guam. They brought the following with them:

- 22 crates of cash valued at $717 million
- 300 crates of assorted fine jewelry
- $4 million worth of unset precious gems shoved in Pampers diaper boxes
- 65 Seiko and Cartier watches
- A 12-by-4-foot box crammed full of real pearls
- A 3-foot solid gold statue covered in diamonds and other precious stones
- $200,000 in gold bullion and nearly $1 million in Philippine pesos
- Deposit slips to banks in the U.S., Switzerland, and the Cayman Islands worth $124 million

After three years in Hawaii, Marcos died of kidney, heart, and lung ailments, 17 days after his 72nd birthday.

During their time in Hawaii, he and Imelda lived in a luxurious house in Makiki Heights. They were known worldwide for hosting costly parties while back in the Philippines the people suffered under the debt the Marcos family had incurred during their rule.

As president from 1986 to 1992, Cory Aquino oversaw the drafting of the 1987 Constitution, which limited the powers of the presidency and reestablished the bicameral

Congress, successfully removing the previous dictatorial government structure. Although unpopular, she paid off much of the Marcos's debts to improve foreign trust and relations.

At the end of her term, she quietly returned to civilian life. Following her death on August 1, 2009, monuments and public landmarks were named in her honor through-out the Philippines. Known in her country as the *Mother of Democracy*, Cory Aquino had become her Future Self. She had fulfilled her purpose.

There are Seven Truths about your Future Self.

We all have a future ahead of us. In 10 years, 20 years, and more, we will become our Future Selves.

The question is: Who will your Future Self be?

What life will you live?

What will you commit yourself to?

As Cory did, you will find your Future Self is often far different than you expect. Cory could have never predicted she would succeed Marcos as the first female president.

We all change. Life events change us.

Aging changes us.

Learning, relationships, experience, success, and failure changes us.

As you learn these seven core truths, you'll be equipped to handle the changes you'll experience in life. You'll also have the skills to choose and create proactive change for yourself and others.

TRUTH #1

YOUR FUTURE DRIVES YOUR PRESENT

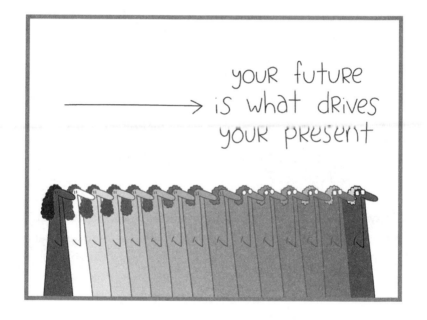

"It is absurd to suppose that purpose is not present because we do not observe the agent deliberating."

—Aristotle[4]

The philosopher Aristotle believed that understanding the nature of causes was fundamental to a successful investigation of the world around us. In one of Plato's best-known dialogues called *Phaedo,* or *On the Soul*, Plato stated that an "inquiry into nature" consists in a search for "the causes of each thing; why each thing comes into existence, why it goes out of existence, why it exists."[5]

Aristotle formulated what are now known as the four causes, which he used to explain how the world works. The fourth of his causes is used to explain human behavior and is called *final cause*, which he defined as "the end, that for the sake of which a thing is done."[6,7,8,9]

All behavior is done for an end.

Final cause is based on teleology. The word *télos* means "the end or cause of a thing."[10] According to teleology, all human behavior is goal or future driven, the means to some end. The goal or end is the cause of the behavior. Health, for example, is the end of walking, losing weight, seeing the doctor, and eating well.

Aristotle used final cause to explain the difference between humans and other life forms. Animals are reactive and instinctual in their actions, the direct byproduct of their environments and impulses. Humans, on the other hand, are intelligent for the very reason that we can consciously choose our actions and behaviors based on desired ends and outcomes.

For Aristotle, all intelligent human action is *intentional*, and based on sought after causes or ends. We can envision and choose goals, and direct our behavior at our goals. Indeed, our goals are the cause of what we do.

Every intelligent action is toward an aim. For example, does a house get built by random chance, or because there was an aim to build it? Moreover, how could you know the process and materials needed to build the house without a blueprint? What is the purpose of this house? Is it for a large or small family? Is the purpose for a group home or a home office?

Do you randomly hammer wood together and hope a house appears, or is there intelligent design? Is a Rolex watch accidental or created? How does someone finish college, build a business, write a book, or ride a bike? Is it by design or random chance?

Isn't the goal what determines the process?

Doesn't mental creation precede physical creation, to use Covey's language?

How could you assemble a rocket and fly to the moon without wanting to do so?

Every human creation you see is the byproduct of intelligent design. Someone had an idea for creating something, and turned their idea into a physical form. This process is trial and error, but driven by a goal.

Look around. Whatever you see is intelligent design.

The clothes you wear. Even this book began as an idea before I started writing. Along the way, I imagined the structure and put words on the page. The book wasn't finished until I felt it matched my vision of what it could be. None of the process happened randomly. I didn't just wake up and have a book written. The ideas and structure of this title are a conscious organization of previously disorganized thoughts, quotes, research, and stories.

Creativity occurs by giving form or organization to disorganized raw materials. For example, a table isn't built out of nothing but organized from raw materials that were previously disorganized or undesigned. Wood, stone, nails, and glue are brought together to form a table. In the case of wood, the material began as a tree, was disassembled from that form into a new form as lumber. After thought and planning, the lumber was reorganized into furniture.

Creation is the intelligent organization of raw materials into a specific form. Creation, or intelligent design, doesn't exist without a specific goal or aim. Ralph Waldo Emerson said, "Shallow men believe in luck . . . Strong men believe in cause and effect."

This brings up a fundamental question you and I must answer for ourselves, and that is, do you believe life is random or can it be designed? Do you believe your behavior and situation are random, or influenced and shaped?

I recently brought this question to my wife, and pointed to the baseball cap she wore. "Was it an intentional decision to put that hat on your head, or did it just happen?"

"I really wasn't thinking," she replied. "I was cleaning the house, saw the hat, and put it on to keep my hair out of my face."

"But did the hat get on your head randomly, or did you put it on? Was there a moment in time, even if only a split second, when you decided to grab the hat and put it on your head?"

"Yes, but the action was more automatic than thoughtful."

"Agreed, but if you didn't want the hat on your head, would it have gotten there?"

Every behavior, even if small and mostly subconscious, is for an end. The billionaire Peter Thiel asks, "If you believe your life is mainly a matter of chance, then why read this book?" Thiel then says:

You can expect the future to take a definite form or you can treat it as hazily uncertain. If you treat your future as something definite, it makes sense to understand it in advance and to work to shape it. But if you expect an indefinite future ruled by randomness, you will give up trying to master it.[11]

According to Thiel, there are indefinite attitudes and definite attitudes about the future:

Indefinite attitudes to the future explain what's most dysfunctional in our world today. Process trumps substance: when people lack concrete plans to carry out, they use formal rules to assemble a portfolio of various options . . . A definite view, by contrast, favors firm convictions. Instead of pursuing many-sided mediocrity and calling it "well-roundedness," a definite person determines the one best thing to do and then does it.

In the modern self-help world, there has been a shift from definite attitudes about the future to indefinite attitudes. Reflected in this ethos is a trend against intelligent design and goal-setting. The common arguments assume that you cannot control any of the outcomes in your life, and therefore you should ignore or forget them.

Although well intentioned and intellectually interesting, the advice to forget about goals is ultimately dishonest. The authors presenting these views don't reflect their teachings in their actions. It's impossible to live life in a purely process-driven and systematic way without any respect for outcomes.

Take for example James Clear, who argues in his book *Atomic Habits* we should "forget about setting goals" and that "true long-term thinking is goal-less thinking."[12] Yet when asked directly, he ultimately conceded that goals are the driver. In an interview on the *School of Greatness* podcast, Lewis Howes asked Clear, "What are the five non-negotiable habits for you, on a daily basis?" to which Clear answered, "So, obviously this is going to depend on your goals," and then shared some of his personal habits.[13] He later wrote that "If you genuinely care about the goal, you'll focus on the system."[14]

Behavior becomes more intelligent as it is intentionally designed for ends.

Einstein said, "Insanity is doing the same thing over and over and expecting a different result." If you completely ignore your results, and continue doing your process, how can you know your process works? You couldn't.

Even flow, which by all accounts is a total absorption in the process, requires clear goals.[15] As Mihaly Csikszentmihalyi, the lead researcher and scholar on flow, has said,

> Flow tends to occur when the activity one engages in contains a clear set of goals. These goals serve to add direction and purpose to behavior.[16]

Without specified goals, flow is extremely difficult because goals create constraints within which a person can focus. If you have absolutely no objectives for your day, how could you possibly know where to focus?

Specific goals are a vital flow trigger. As Steven Kotler, one of the leading experts on flow, stated, "What's critical is we know what we're doing now and we know what we're doing next, so attention can stay focused in the present."[17]

Goals create the constraints that guide us. Flow most easily occurs as you break big goals down to their smallest chunk. If you're a football team, rather than overly focusing on the goal to win the game, you simplify the focus to the set of downs, and even to the specific play. Rather than trying to win the game, you try to get the touchdown, or the next first down. That's the mile marker.

Focus on the goal right in front of you, and do that again and again, knowing these are the critical steps to the overarching goal of winning the game, and then the championship.

If you're a writer, rather than focusing on the completion of the whole book, you simplify the goal to a single chapter, a single illustration, a single page, a single paragraph.

In order to be in a flow state, it is essential to focus on one goal at a time. Multitasking interrupts flow. For instance, try to have a conversation while checking email. That's two goals. No flow.

The core truth of humanity is that all human behavior is driven by goals. To Frankl, this was the ultimate and eternal truth. As he stated, "It is a peculiarity of man that he can only live by looking to the future-*sub specie aeternitatis*. And this is his salvation in the most difficult moments of his existence."[18]

Every human action, even my wife hastily putting on her hat, is goal-driven. Many, if not most, goals are reactive to one's environment or situation. The more intentional and proactive you become in your actions, goals, and thinking, the more intelligent and freer you'll be.

Truth #1 is that your future drives your present.

Human beings are intelligent to the extent they are intentional, conscious, and honest about the goals that are driving them.

YOUR FUTURE SELF IS DIFFERENT THAN YOU EXPECT

"Human beings are works in progress that mistakenly think they're finished. The person you are right now is as transient, as fleeting and as temporary as all the people you've ever been."

—Dr. Daniel Gilbert[19]

Dr. Daniel Gilbert is a Harvard psychologist who has studied the Future Self concept for nearly 20 years. In 2006, he published a book titled *Stumbling Upon Happiness*, wherein he explains his research that people imagine the future poorly, especially their view of what will make them happy.[20] In 2014, he gave a mainstage TED Talk entitled *The Psychology of Your Future Self*.[21]

Gilbert has a unique way of discovering errors in people's thinking regarding their Future Selves. "Think ten years ago," Gilbert begins. "Are you today the exact same person you were ten years ago?"

Considering who they were, what their lives were like, and what they were focused on, people quickly discern they've changed a lot over the previous decade.

Their interests are different.

Their perspectives, values, and circumstances changed.

Their focus and goals changed.

In many instances, what was important ten years ago is no longer relevant to who they are today.

After having people examine the differences between their current and former selves, Gilbert asked them to think about their Future Self. "Do you think you'll be much different ten years from now, from who you are today?"

Despite acknowledging major changes in themselves over the previous 10 years, people consistently assume only minor changes in themselves over the upcoming decade. Gilbert explains:

At every age, people underestimate how much their personalities will change in the next decade. And it isn't just ephemeral things like values and personality. You can ask people about their likes and dislikes, their basic preferences. For example, name your best friend, your favorite kind of vacation, what's your favorite hobby, what's your favorite kind of music . . . To give you an idea of the magnitude of this effect . . . 18-year-olds anticipate changing only as much as 50-year-olds actually do.[22]

People tend to assume that who they are right now is, for the most part, the finished version. We feel like who we are now is who we truly are, and who we'll mostly be. We might change a little, but not much. Our current self is the real us.

Psychologists call this the *end-of-history illusion*.[23,24] It's the belief that you've substantially changed in the past, but likely won't change much in the future. It is common to assume that your Future Self will mostly be the same person as you are today. Gilbert explained a core reason for this is likely due to "the ease of remembering and the difficulty of imagining." As he continues:

> Most of us can remember who we were 10 years ago, but we find it hard to imagine who we're going to be, and then we mistakenly think that because it's hard to imagine, it's not likely to happen. Sorry, when people say, "I can't imagine that," they're usually talking about their own lack of imagination, and not about the unlikelihood of the event that they're describing.

Another term for the belief that your current and Future Self are essentially the same person is what esteemed psychologist Dr. Carol Dweck called *the fixed mindset*.[25] According to Dweck:

In a fixed mindset, people believe their basic qualities, like their intelligence or talent, are simply fixed traits. They spend their time documenting their intelligence or talent instead of developing them.

People with a fixed mindset have an utter lack of imagination about themselves. Due to their lack of confidence, people with a fixed mindset have a fragile identity, relentlessly avoiding any forms of failure. From their fixed perspective, if they fail, then what must that failure say about them?

People with a fixed mindset overemphasize and overly define their current selves, believing who they are now is their core self. Unchangeable and innate, their inner dialogue states, "This is who I am and who I'm always going to be."

Dr. Gilbert's research highlights that most people have a fairly fixed mindset about themselves. Most people assume their Future Self won't be much different from their current

self. In fact, if a stranger could have a conversation with the person you were 10 years ago, and the person you are today, they'd be talking to two totally different people. Your Future Self will be just as different.

As discussed in Threat #4, a crucial aspect of connecting with your Future Self is seeing them as a *different person*. Dr. Gilbert's research helps us realize that our Future Self will be far different than we expect, even without conscious effort on our part.

Your Future Self is a totally different person than you are today.

They see the world differently.

They have different goals and concerns than you now have.

They have a different situation.

They have different habits.

They even have a different way of looking at the world.

They've been through experiences and learned things you simply can't comprehend.

It is not only accurate to see your Future Self as a different person, it's crucial to living effectively.

When you see your Future Self as a different person, you don't get stuck or dogmatic in your current way of thinking. You love your current self, and appreciate how temporary your current perspectives, attributes, and situation are.

You will change and evolve. This is freeing and exciting. Knowing you can and will change enables you to love your current self. You're less rigid about how you see yourself. You don't need all the answers right now. You don't need to prove your current capability or worth.

Your current self is temporary. This refreshing truth enables a growth mindset, where you're more interested in learning and growing than trying to prove yourself. It creates a flexible identity, where you actively update and alter your perspectives, and continually upgrade how you think, what you measure, and what you value.

The promise of change empowers you to give grace to your current self. You can make mistakes. It's okay that you don't have all the answers. It's okay if you're a bit disorganized and camped in the messy middle. Things will change. If you're committed to a certain change or outcome, then you will figure it out.

This truth helps in my current life. In many ways, I am neck-deep in the messy middle. Even writing this book, for a really long time felt like a total dumpster fire. I could see the completed book in my mind, but the reality of creating the work felt hard and sometimes painful. I'm in the messy middle in so many other areas of my life as a father, with my health, and building my finances.

And you know what? I'm completely happy with this! I know my current self and situation are temporary. I know that a week from now, I'll see things differently. I'll be in a different place.

I'm not stuck, and neither are you.

Your trajectory matters far more than your current position.

Truth #2 is that your Future Self is far different than you expect them to be. Visit futureself.com to access the *Future Self Imagination Tool*. This tool allows you to see how different your current self is from your former self. Additionally, you'll be able to project how different your Future Self will be 10 years in the future.

Albert Einstein correctly said, "Imagination is more important than knowledge."[26] When you appreciate that your Future Self will be a totally different person than you are today, then you free yourself of needing to be perfect or finished now.

Your current self is radically temporary and fleeting.

You'll even be different tomorrow.

Let this truth free you. Enhance the compassion, empathy, and love you have for your current self, as well as your former and Future Self.

TRUTH #3

YOUR FUTURE SELF IS THE PIED PIPER

"Time will be your friend or your enemy; it will promote you or expose you."

—Jeff Olson[27]

Paying the piper is a phrase that means suffering the consequences of your own self-indulgent actions. The most accepted origin of this phrase is the legend dating back to the Middle Ages of the Pied Piper of Hamelin. The citizens of Hamelin had a plague of rats. When the Pied Piper offered to get rid of them for a sum of money, they accepted his offer.

With his pipe, the Piper led the rats away, but the citizens refused to pay. To punish them, the Piper enticed their children away with his music and imprisoned them in a hill forever.

The point of this parable? Everything you do has a consequence for better or worse. Everything you do has a compounding consequence. Your Future Self is the exaggerated result of your current decisions.

In reality, the Pied Piper *is* your Future Self. The Pied Piper *will* be paid.

You can't escape your Future Self. You can't escape paying the Piper. The only choice you have is, *when* will you pay the Piper, and *how* much?

Author Jim Rohn, said, "Discipline weighs ounces while regret weighs tons."

Discipline costs dollars. Regret costs millions. This same principle applies to paying your Future Self.

If you pay the Pied Piper every single day, by making small and consistent *investments*, you'll get a massive bargain. Every time you invest in your Future Self, you've not only paid them, but you've invested in them. By investing in your Future Self, your Future Self continually gets bigger and better.

The reverse is to continually borrow from your Future Self, and wait until some future time to pay them back. A cost to your Future Self is anything that has more downsides than upsides. Generally, a cost is some short-term reward or indulgence that has no positive aftereffects, and often has negative consequences.

Reactive behavior is usually costly.

The more you put your Future Self in debt in terms of health, learning, finances, and time, the more painful and costly will be the eventual toll. There will be a lot of interest to pay if you continually accrue debt.

Everything you do can be categorized as either a cost to or an investment in your Future Self.

Costing your Future Self means you're more focused on present or short-term rewards over long-term consequences. Costing your Future Self means you're consuming far more than you're creating.

Every little action adds up. A cost makes you less healthy in some way, whether mentally, emotionally, spiritually, relationally, or physically. If repeated, costs make you fatter, lazier, hazier, and less connected. A cost is something that comes to control you, rather than you controlling it.

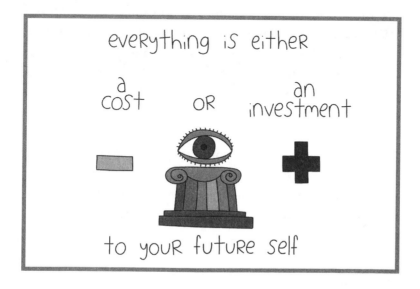

In the 1990s, the chip company Pringles had a catch-line referencing their pop-off lids, "Once you pop, the fun don't stop!"

Costs are heavily addictive. Have you ever tried just eating one chip? It's essentially torture. Most people, once they pop open the cannister and eat one chip, can't stop.

The same is true of all mindless and costly behavior. Once you pop, you can't stop. For example, if you open your phone to reactively or randomly check some input, you're going to addictively continue that behavior repeatedly throughout the day.

Pop, pop, pop.

Cost, cost, cost.

Reactively opening your smartphone at the beginning of the day is akin to grabbing that first chip. You've just put yourself into consumption mode and there will never be enough to consume, because the rewards are so short-lived.

To see the situation differently, imagine your cell phone as a chip that is making your Future Self fatter. Every time you engage in costly myopic decision-making, remember that you're eating a chip. Once you pop, the fun don't stop.

The opposite of costing your Future Self with short-term rewards is investing in your Future Self. Rather than putting your Future Self in deeper debt, make your Future Self wealthier. Continually position your Future Self for freedom of time, money, relationships, and overall sense of purpose.

An investment toward your Future Self is any conscious action you're making toward chosen goals. Every time you consciously invest in something specific, whether learning, health, relationships, or experiences, your Future Self grows more capable, free, and mature.

Every investment compounds over time, making your Future Self wealthier. The earlier you invest, the more your Future Self compounds.

Albert Einstein is attributed with saying:

Compound interest is the eighth wonder of the world. He who understands it, earns it . . . he who doesn't . . . pays it.

The compound effect refers to how small changes compound into dramatic results. It's the ripple effect you get from the choices you make. In life, you not only reap what you sow, you reap more than you sow.

Everything compounds over time. Little things become big things, for better or worse. Reading one good book may not change your life. But that one book could lead to the next book, and the next, and the next. Your knowledge and perspectives compound, creating unpredictable changes and results. Over time, you become a different person, and the process started with one book.

Your Future Self is the compounded effect of your actions now.

Your Future Self is more exaggerated than you think. The size and potential of your Future Self are way beyond what you're probably thinking. Realize the potential of your Future Self and you immediately increase the value of your current self.

One dollar today may be worth $20, $50, and more to your Future Self, which your Future Self invests to make $500, $1,000, and more. Suddenly the dollar in your hand has unlimited value.

A seed in the hands of your current self may be a massive oak tree in the backyard of your Future Self. An idea in your mind today may be a company or movement changing the world in the tomorrow.

But there's far more to the compound effect than accelerated growth.

Plant a seed today and your Future Self will have more than a single tree. There will be many additional benefits or byproducts of planting that single tree that your current self could never predict. Maybe, after you planted that first tree, you recognize the good trees do for the Earth. You plant thousands of trees, which grow into orchards and forests. While your orchard is growing, your Future Self learns about land and agriculture and your farms yield food for millions of people every year.

All because you planted one seed.

If you invested $50 per week in the stock market, you'd build your portfolio. Initially, $50 seems inconsequential. But after six months, the balance totals $300. This may be the most money you've ever accumulated in your life.

This then impacts your identity capital. You identify yourself as someone who invests and can grow your income. A meta-analysis showed that confidence is the byproduct of prior success.[28] Seeing small wins, your confidence grows, which expands your imagination for what you could do in the future.

If I can get to $300, I can probably get to $3,000. If I can get to $3,000, I can probably get to $300,000.

As your confidence grows, your motivation expands. Because you believe you can succeed, and because your vision keeps growing, your motivation is ignited to create exciting results.

The primary challenge most people face is that they never invest, or start investing way too late.

Another challenge people face is that they're unwilling to start really small. When it comes to goals, you want to have a massive vision. When taking action, break the goal into the smallest possible unit.

Dr. BJ Fogg, the Stanford behavior scientist and author of *Tiny Habits*, found that tiny is how you create habits.[29] To become successful, you'll eventually invest really big. But to get there, start small.

Many people are unwilling to start small. They're unwilling to be a beginner or novice.

Start investing a little bit in your Future Self, whatever that means to you. Place $20 in crypto. Buy that $11 book. Push your body for 30 minutes at the gym. Begin investing in the areas you want to compound.

In 2015, during the first year of my Ph.D. program, I set out on my path to become a professional writer. After talking to literary agents and professional authors, I realized I'd need to grow an audience before I could get a publisher. So, I started blogging. I found an online course for $198 by a guy named John Morrow. With my wife's blessing, because this was an expensive investment for our former selves, I made the purchase and learned how to create viral headlines and article structures, and pitch my articles onto platforms like *Forbes* and *Psychology Today*.

It wasn't a crazy investment. But that investment got me committed and gave me the capability and confidence to blog successfully. I dove in and wrote 50 articles in the first few months. Most of those pieces were pretty bad and didn't get many views. However, by continually applying what I learned, and through deliberate practice, it only took a few months to write my first viral article, which received over 20 million views.

Small investments lead to bigger investments.

The more you invest, the more those investments compound.

Investing gets you committed.

Investing gets you results.

Investing is how you proactively upgrade your vision and goals. As you invest in yourself, you increase your commitment to a bigger vision. This change in commitment simultaneously alters your identity, since your identity is what you're most committed to.[30]

During my Ph.D. program in industrial and organizational psychology, I examined the differences between wannabe entrepreneurs and successful ones. What was the difference? Was there an inflection point for the successful entrepreneurs, where they transitioned from wannabes to 100 percent committed?

Was there a point of no return? And if so, what occurred after that point of no return?

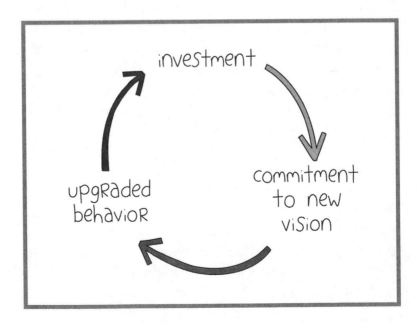

Those were the questions of my master's thesis: *Does It Take Courage to Start a Business?*[31]

My research proved there was a point of no return. Even the wannabe entrepreneurs believed they may, at some future point, pass that moment. Still committed to being employees, they hadn't gotten there yet.

The point of no return occurred the moment a person got 100 percent committed to their objective of being an entrepreneur. It was an identity shift. That moment of deci sion was usually initiated by making a financial *investment* in their business.

My favorite narrative was a high school entrepreneur who, with his friend, invested their life savings into a shipment of shoes they planned to sell. It was about a $10,000 investment, and it terrified them.

Once the delivery truck dropped the mountain of shoes at his house, he knew there was no going back. Immediately, his identity changed, and he locked into his goal of succeeding as an entrepreneur. In his own words:

> Yeah, once we had all of our money in the same inventory it was all or nothing. That really scared me, just knowing that it was like do or die. I had to sell the shoes. You couldn't turn back; you couldn't just get rid of them and get cash back; you had to go forward.

I asked, "Did anything change after this moment?"

> After that, once I realized that we were truly going and everything, it really just opened me up to what I was able to do. At that point, I was like, okay, I actually started a company. I've invested in it, and

now I need to run this thing. That's when I think I really saw that I was running the company. It really changed my leadership role with my partners.

By getting invested, he got committed. Then, his identity changed. From there, he took up that leadership role with far more elevated and bold behavior, which led to his success.

Before getting invested, he wasn't 100 percent committed to succeeding in this particular venture. He had entertained the idea and grown more interested. But before paying his money, he was committed to whatever else he was doing with his time. Once invested, he became fully committed to a singular focus. With his new commitment, his identity aligned with that commitment, and his behavior followed his new identity.

This is how you proactively change and elevate your vision. By upgrading your vision, you change your identity and behavior.

The more you invest, the more committed you'll be.

The more you invest, the bigger your vision will be.

Invest your time, your money, and your talents.

Investing is how you shatter the glass ceiling of your current potential and elevate your sense of what you can be and do. This profound behavior signals to your subconscious that you can have and be much more than your current identity.[32] As Dr. David Hawkins stated, "The unconscious will only allow us to have what we believe we deserve."[33]

Truth #3 is that your Future Self is the Pied Piper. You can pay yourself now or put your Future Self in debt.

Either way, the Piper will be paid.

Start investing now. Then, make bigger and bigger investments.

Your Future Self will thank you.

THE MORE VIVID AND DETAILED YOUR FUTURE SELF, THE FASTER YOU'LL PROGRESS

"What preoccupies us is the way we define success."
—Arianna Huffington[34]

"You see whatever it is you're measuring."
—Seth Godin[35]

My 14-year-old son, Kaleb, is an avid tennis player. In addition to three to five lessons per week, he competes in multiple tournaments every month. But for almost a year, he lost most of his tournaments despite extensive practice and often being far more skilled than his competitors.

Recently, Kaleb's coach took him aside and asked about his tennis future. "You have potential. Do you want to play in college?"

He told Kaleb about a tennis academy that would help him achieve a skill level where he could play in college. To attend this higher-level academy, Kaleb needed to raise his Universal Tennis Ranking (UTR) to a three. UTR is a scale from 1 to 16.5.

Kaleb and I learned the UTR system, looked up top pros, and studied players at colleges he might want to attend. As of January 4, 2022, Novak Djokovic is the #1 tennis player in the world and has a UTR of 16.26. Serena Williams is the #2 ranked female in the United States, and has a 12.93 UTR.

Over the next two months, Kaleb brought his UTR from 1.4 to 2.8.

Kaleb knows that to get into his desired colleges, he needs to get his UTR to a 9. He has a clear next mile marker of raising his UTR to a 3 so he can attend the academy.

Once Kaleb had a clear goal and measuring process, he won nine matches in a row. He had a reason to win. Each match impacted his UTR score. Having clear measurables and milestones motivated Kaleb to become enormously more effective in how he practiced, and strategic in which tournaments he played.

In the past, Kaleb's measuring process wasn't tied to his tournament play, as well as being connected to his long-term Future Self. Kaleb now envisions his Future Self playing in college with a UTR above 10. His Future Self is vivid, detailed, and measurable.

With the clear objective of getting his UTR to a 3, a measuring system to gauge his progress, and a reason to get serious in his tournaments, it's like a switch flipped.

He wanted to win.

Truth #4 is that the more measurable and detailed your Future Self, the faster you'll progress toward your goals. Effective progress comes with a combination of measurable metrics, a vivid vision of your Future Self, and clear mile markers. Without these elements, people wander.

In fact, it is so commonly depicted that people who are lost wander in circles that researchers tested the common theme found in books and movies. Do people walk in circles when they lack clear direction?

Scientists at the Max Planck Institute for Biological Cybernetics took participants to a thick forest and gave simple instructions, "Walk in a straight line."

Without distinguishable landmarks to guide them, test subjects had to rely only on their sense of direction and their ability to put one foot in front of the other.

When questioned afterward, several participants were confident they'd not deviated at all. Yet, despite their confidence, GPS data showed that they walked in loops as tight as 20 meters in diameter.[36] As it turned out, "People really [do] walk in circles when they do not have reliable cues to their walking direction."[37]

One initial theory as to why they walked in circles was that people must have one leg longer than the other, which causes a slight deviation in walking over time. This idea proved false because often the same people when tested multiple times would walk in circles to the right, and other times circles to the left.

Walking in circles wasn't due to leg length, but rather, as the researchers of the study explained, was "the result of increasing uncertainty about where straight ahead is."[38]

The study concluded that without clarity of where straight is, you'll wander in circles despite thinking you're making progress forward. Without a clear goal for yourself, and tangible mile markers along the way, you'll wander in circles.

The more vivid, detailed, and measurable your Future Self, the easier to become your Future Self.

The Japanese skateboarder Yuto Horigome is a great example of following a detailed and measurable Future Self. From 2017–2021, Yuto went from an average pro skater to the top ranked skater in the world.

Yuto started skateboarding seriously in 2010 at age 11. By 2013, he had gained recognition as one of the top skateboarders in Japan. However, he knew the level of

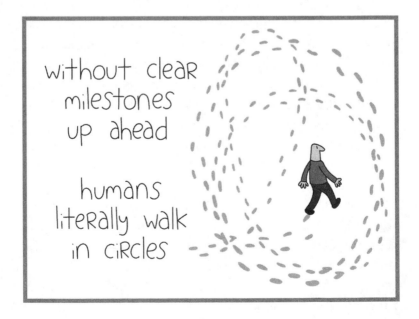

without cleaR
milestones
up ahead

humans
liteRally walk
in ciRcles

skateboarding in Japan was far behind America, so in 2014, at age 15, he entered skate contests in the United States. At 17 years old, Yuto moved to California, the world's mecca for skateboarding. He left his family to fulfill his dream of becoming a pro skater. Though he entered big contests, after a year of competing he had not come close to a win.

Yuto thought about why he was struggling. He realized he did the same tricks as the American skateboarders. There was nothing distinctive about his style. He decided to master the fundamentals of skateboarding with utter precision and consistency beyond the level anyone had mastered before. He developed his own style, and invented tricks no one else did to stand out in competitions.

Pablo Picasso said, "Learn the rules like a pro, so you can break them like an artist."

From 2016 to 2019, Yuto blocked out lesser goals and got laser focused. As he stated in an interview, "Honestly, the daily practice helped me a lot."[39]

Yuto recalled his vision of his Future Self he'd written in his elementary school yearbook "to become the best skateboarder in the world."[40] To accomplish his goal required becoming a master craftsman as a skateboarder.

He invested hours imagining innovative tricks and practiced executing the feats with style. Watching Yuto skateboard is a visual feast of practice, precision, and intelligent design. The tricks are polished, technical, and performed seamlessly.

During the years of extreme focus and deliberate practice, Yuto competed constantly. He started winning, and surged from an unknown skater to becoming globally famous. He went from having an average skate style to succeeding as one of the most elite and unique contest skaters.

He won gold in the 2019 X Games in Minnesota and became the second ranked skateboarder in the world. Next, he shifted his focus to the 2020 Tokyo Olympics.

The 2020 Olympics would be the first time that skateboarding would be an Olympic sport. However, due to the COVID-19 pandemic, the Olympics were pushed to 2021. Yuto took advantage of the additional time to train and invent new routines.

As the Olympics neared in July of 2021, Yuto had captured the attention of the entire skateboarding world. Despite being ranked second and the underdog behind the American skateboarder, Nyjah Huston, when the competition began Yuto seemed far more grounded than Huston.

Yuto was rock-solid consistent.

His tricks looked decades ahead of the other skateboarders.

His style was precise.

Yuto won and became the hometown hero for bringing Olympic gold to his country. What made the medal even more special was that Yuto grew up near the Ariake Urban Sports Park, where the Olympic events were held.

He'd fulfilled his childhood dream.

Yuto succeeded because he created with extreme detail and craftsmanship. Not only did he see himself becoming the best in the world, but he invented the most technical, challenging, and beautiful performance seen on a skateboard.

His goal shaped his process. And he committed to that process until he won Olympic Gold.

Truth #4 is that the detail and vividness of your Future Self determines your ability to achieve it. The more detailed your Future Self, the better. The more measurable and specific your goals and milestones, the more effective will be your process and progress.

TRUTH #5

FAILING AS YOUR FUTURE SELF IS BETTER THAN SUCCEEDING AS YOUR CURRENT SELF

"In time with years of creative training and a willingness to invest in loss, to take blow after blow and get blasted off the pedestals as a way of life, the game starts to slow down. You see attacks coming in slow motion and play refutational maneuvers in the blink of an eye."

—Josh Waitzkin[41]

One day while walking with his mom through Washington Square Park in New York City, Josh Waitzkin noticed people playing chess. Only 6 years old, Josh became immediately gripped by the game.

He played in the park with the street players, and at age 7, worked with his first formal teacher, Bruce Pandolfini. At age 10, Josh sacrificed his queen and rook in exchange for a checkmate six moves later and his first victory against a master ranked player, Edward Frumkin.

At age 15, he earned the title of National Master, and at 16 became an International Master.

In 1988, when Josh was 12 years old, his father, Fred Waitzkin, published a book about Josh called *Searching for Bobby Fischer*. That story became a major motion picture film when Josh was 17 and at the top of the chess world. Though chess is not commonly a spectator sport, crowds turned out to watch him play.

For Josh, the fans were distracting, and the fame and pressure to win mounted. He left America and chess to pursue meditation, philosophy, and tai chi. In his book, *The Art of Learning: An Inner Journey to Optimal Performance*, Josh shares the principle of "investment in loss" he applied to eventually become the 2004 world champion in Taiji Push Hands, a competitive martial form of tai chi.[42]

When he first focused on Push Hands, Josh proactively trained with others who were multiple skill levels ahead of him. For Josh, *"investment in loss"* is "giving yourself to the learning process." This means putting yourself in difficult situations that force you to adapt. Facing your weaknesses. And sometimes, literally, using Josh's words, getting "thrown around."

For Josh, "investing in loss" was an extreme form of *deliberate practice*. According to Dr. Anders Ericsson, the lead researcher on deliberate practice and expert performance, deliberate practice is meant to counter our natural inclination to develop habits or "automaticity," which is the ability to perform a task without conscious effort.[43]

For certain tasks like tying our shoes and driving, automaticity is fantastic because it frees up our mind to do other things. However, when it comes to developing skills and learning, automaticity is how you get stuck at a certain skill level, and slowly decline over time.[44]

For example, research shows that doctors who have been in practice for 20 years are usually less skilled than they were fresh out of medical school. These older doctors are stuck in habitual ways of thinking and acting, and haven't updated their models or approaches for years. Rather than having 20 years of experience, they often have 1 year of experience repeated 20 times.[45] As Dr. Ericsson stated:

> After some limited training and experience—frequently less than 50 hours for most recreational activities, such as skiing, tennis, and driving a car—an individual's performance is adapted to the typical situational demands and is increasingly automated, and they lose conscious control over aspects of their behavior and are no longer able to make specific intentional adjustments. For example, people have automated how they tie their shoelaces or how they stand up from sitting in a chair. When performance has reached this level of automaticity and effortless execution, additional experience will not improve the accuracy of behavior nor refine the structure of the mediating mechanisms, and consequently, the amount of accumulated experience will not be related to higher levels of performance. In direct contrast,

aspiring experts continue to improve their performance as a function of more experience because it
is coupled with deliberate practice. The key challenge for aspiring expert performers is to avoid the
arrested development associated with automaticity.
These individuals purposefully counteract tendencies
toward automaticity by actively setting new goals and
higher performance standards, which require them
to increase speed, accuracy, and control over their
actions. The experts deliberately construct and seek
out training situations to attain desired goals that
exceed their current level of reliable performance.[46]

Deliberate practice is the opposite of "habits" or "automaticity." Your habits are you on autopilot. Deliberate practice
requires conscious effort and attention toward specific and
challenging goals. Habits are your current self; deliberate practice is focused striving toward your desired Future Self. Revert-
ing to habits or your comfort zone isn't how you advance.

Josh's "investment in loss" strategy is the ultimate form
of deliberate practice. He explains how he specifically applied
"investment in loss" to learn Push Hands against an overly
aggressive man named Evan, whom he describes as "Six-
foot-two, 200-pound second-degree karate blackbelt, eight-
year Aikido student, and an eight-year student of Tai Chi."

Josh described:

> When he came at me, my whole body braced for
> impact. I had no idea how to function from relax-
> ation when a freight train was leveling me fifty
> times a night. I felt like a punching bag. Basically, I
> had two options—I could avoid Evan or get beat up
> every class. I spent many months getting smashed

around by Evan, and admittedly it was not easy to invest in loss when I was being pummeled against walls. I'd limp home from practice.

With this nontraditional approach, Josh was failing at the level of his Future Self rather than succeeding at the level of his current self. When given free training time, the other students in Master Chen's class proactively matched themselves with people at or below their own skill level. Because the other students weren't purposefully putting themselves through constant and painful failure like Josh, he advanced much faster than his peers. He adapted up to the skills of those he trained with.

The other students weren't willing to invest in loss to the same degree as Josh. They were comfortable succeeding at their current level rather than failing at their Future Self level. And for good reason. Deliberate practice, when taken seriously, is extremely painful.

To fully engage in deliberate practice is to have an increasingly clear picture of your desired Future Self. As Dr. Thomas Suddendorf, Dr. Melissa Brinums, and Dr. Kana Imuta, three of the top researchers on prospection and Future Self stated:

> Only through imaging a Future Self with improved skills may we be able to motivate, plan, and execute the honing of skills through deliberate practice.[47]

Josh also believes in the importance of being clear on what you want. He is considered by many to be one of the world's leading experts on learning and high performance. "I've come to realize that what I'm best at is not Tai Chi, and it is not chess," he said. "What I'm best at is the art of learning."[48]

A child chess prodigy, Josh became a world champion. He also became world champion in tai chi and Brazilian Jiu Jitsu. He trains people who are world class at what they do to reach the top one percent of the top one percent of their respective field or art. At the foundation of Josh's methods are approaches for realizing one's Future Self.

In two separate interviews with Tim Ferriss in 2020 and 2021, Josh spoke at length about his process of proactively connecting with and getting advice from his own Future Self.[49,50] As Josh explains in the 2020 interview:

> No one will know me better than myself 20 years from now. If my goal is unobstructed self-expression or self-actualization within an art, then the person who's teaching me should be the person who knows me most deeply. And that's me 20 years from now.[51]

Being connected with his Future Self is what enables Josh to continually invest in loss. He's connected to a much more evolved version of himself. He's committed to his Future Self more than his current comfort. He's aggressive about becoming his Future Self.

Throughout this book, I've used the word *investment* to describe any intentional act toward your desired Future Self. Josh's use of the word *investment* when describing deliberate practice isn't coincidental. For Josh, *investment in loss* was accelerated deliberate learning toward his Future Self. It was his commitment to his Future Self.

Commitment to Future Self means investing in loss or failure here and now to accelerate progress. The more willing you are to invest in momentary loss and pain directed at a goal, the faster you'll adapt to the level of your Future Self.

Truth #5 is that failing as your Future Self is better than succeeding as your current self. This Truth pairs with Threat #6, that being outside the arena will prevent you from learning and progressing.

It's your choice how deep you'll go into the arena.

It's your choice the extent to which you'll invest in loss and learning.

Josh finishes his story with Evan by describing the result of his continuous investment in loss:

> But then a curious thing began to happen. First, as I got used to taking shots from Evan, I stopped fearing the impact . . . Then as I became more relaxed under fire, Evan seemed to slow down in my mind . . . There came a moment when the tables clearly turned for me and Evan. My training had gotten very intense . . . Evan and I hadn't worked together for a while because he started avoiding me as I improved. But this evening Master Chen paired us on the mats. Evan came at me like a bull, and I instinctively avoided his onslaught and threw him on the floor. He got back up, came back at me, and I tossed him again. I was shocked by how easy it felt. After a few minutes of this Evan said that his foot was bothering him, and he called it a night. We shook hands, and he would never work with me again.

If you want to become your desired Future Self, play at their level as quickly as possible. Commit at the level of your Future Self. Adapt at the level of your Future Self. Your current self is clearly not there yet, and will therefore need serious training, humility, and feedback.

People naturally avoid investing in loss. It's comfortable doing something you can already do. Winning feels good. But if you want to aggressively become your Future Self, then investing in loss is how you get there.

SUCCESS IS ACHIEVED BY BEING TRUE TO YOUR FUTURE SELF, NOTHING ELSE

"Chase the future. Live in the world of tomorrow . . . It's the most exciting way to live. Every day will be like a child's birthday, with surprising new breakthroughs. It keeps your brain healthy, young, and active. Since everything will always be new, you won't rely on assumptions or habits. You'll pay full attention and keep learning every day."

—Derek Sivers[52]

"This above all: to thine own self be true."

—William Shakespeare[53]

During the years leading up to and even during World War II, Adolf Hitler was a painter.

In his 1925 autobiography *Mein Kampf,* Hitler described how his childhood dream was to become a professional artist.[54] In 1907, at age 18, Hitler took his inheritance money—700 kronen—and moved to Vienna to study and become an artist. Despite working hard for years on his craft, his dream dashed because he failed the entrance exam of the Academy of Fine Arts Vienna.

Hitler's application to the academy was rejected in 1908 and again in 1909. In his first attempt, he passed the preliminary portion by drawing two of the assigned iconic or biblical scenes, in two sessions of three hours each. However, he failed the second portion of the exam, where examiners reviewed his previously prepared portfolio. The institute considered that he had more talent in architecture than in painting.

He received their rejection as a severe blow and ultimately took his life in a different direction. To quote Steven Pressfield in *The War of Art*:

> You know, Hitler wanted to be an artist . . . Ever see one of his paintings? Neither have I. Resistance beat him. Call it overstatement but I'll say it anyway: it was easier for Hitler to start World War II than it was for him to face a blank square of canvas.[55]

What if Hitler had found another route to becoming a successful artist?

What if he hadn't given up on his desired Future Self?

He couldn't handle the rejection and failure.

He didn't have the hope and pathways thinking to find another way.

He was rigid.

Although he kept producing art throughout his life, it was more of a distraction than the once desired focus of his success.

Shadow Career is the term used to describe people who go on an alternative path from their true dream because they've given up on themselves. To requote Robert Brault, "We are kept from our goals not by obstacles, but by a clear path to a lesser goal."

Though we're talking about one of history's most vile madmen, Hitler's story is an extreme version of many, if not most people's, lives.

Philosopher, entrepreneur, world traveler, and writer Derek Sivers champions strong beliefs about what it means to be *successful*. He believes that it doesn't matter how accomplished you may be, you cannot be considered "a success" unless you are true to what you genuinely want or believe. In a 2015 interview, Tim Ferriss asked, "When you think of the word 'successful,' who's the first person who comes to mind and why?"[56]

Derek responded:

> The first answer to any question isn't much fun because it's just automatic. What's the first painting that comes to mind? Mona Lisa. Name a genius. Einstein. Who's a composer? Mozart. There's the instant, unconscious, automatic thinking and then there's the slower, conscious, rational, deliberate thinking. I'm really, really into the slower thinking, breaking my automatic responses to the things in my life and slowly thinking through a more deliberate response instead.

Derek revised Tim's question.

> What if you asked, "When you think of the word 'successful,' who's the third person that comes to mind? Why are they actually more successful than the first person that came to mind?" In that case, the first would be Richard Branson because he's the stereotype. He's like the Mona Lisa of success to me. Honestly, you [speaking to Tim] might be my second answer, but we could talk about that a different time. My third and real answer, after thinking it through, is that we can't know without knowing a person's aims. What if Richard Branson set out to live a quiet life, but like a compulsive gambler, he just can't stop creating companies? Then that changes everything, and we can't call him successful anymore.

Truth #6 is that success can only be accomplished by being true to your desired Future Self.

Anything less than being true to your Future Self is failure. As you evolve, your view of your Future Self will evolve. Then you'll have a choice, stay on the old path or the new?

Many people appear to be successful, but are actually living a pseudo-version of the life they'd really like to be living. Even Richard Branson couldn't be considered successful if he wasn't actually doing what he truly wanted.

The same can be said of the person living a quiet simple life, that doesn't have fame, money, prestige, or any of the things we often consider as success. If that person is living the life they truly want to live, then *they are absolutely successful*.

External factors are absolutely not what determines if a person is successful or not. Only that a person lives in alignment with their own aims.

TRUTH #7

YOUR VIEW OF GOD IMPACTS YOUR FUTURE SELF

"Our deepest fear is not that we are inadequate. Our deepest fear is that we are powerful beyond measure. It is our light, not our darkness that most frightens us. We ask ourselves, 'Who am I to be brilliant, gorgeous, talented, fabulous?' Actually, who are you not to be? You are a child of God. Your playing small does not serve the world. There is nothing enlightened about shrinking so that other people won't feel insecure around you."

—Marianne Williamson

Let me get this out of the way from the beginning. In this section, I'm *not* in any way attempting to convince you whether or not you *should* believe in God. That choice is fundamentally yours alone.

Instead, the purpose of this section is to highlight how whatever views, or lack of views, you have of God will directly impact your views of your own Future Self.

Whatever view you hold of God largely impacts your views of yourself, your nature, your potential, and your trajectory. Your view of God impacts both your macro and micro views of your own future, both in this life and in a potential afterlife.

For example, if you believe there is a God, and that what you do in this life impacts your state in the next life, then that afterlife future perspective influences your actions today. If you don't believe there is a God, and instead believe there is nothing after this life, then that future perspective will similarly influence your present behavior.

Some perspectives of God leave you with an unclear sense of purpose and a restricted view of your own destiny. From my standpoint, any perspective that limits your Future Self should be questioned, especially when it comes to God.

Other perspectives of God are intensely liberating in respect to your Future Self. In fact, I will share the view I specifically hold of God, and how this vantage point gives me an utterly breath-taking view of not only my own Future Self but also the potential of every other human on this planet.

There are countless views of God and God's relation to humanity. I'm going to detail a few of the classical frameworks. Forgive me for only focusing on a few. My point here isn't to provide a comprehensive list of all the different forms of belief, but to highlight in simple terms the impact of one's beliefs on their own Future Self. From this, I hope to inspire introspection on your own beliefs and their impact on your trajectory.

For instance, a common view is that God controls and determines all things, including all human actions and outcomes. From this view, it doesn't really matter who you are and what you do in this life. God has already predestined who will go to heaven and who will go to hell.

This perspective creates what psychologists call an *external locus of control*, where you believe you have no agency or impact on what happens in your life.[57] It stops you from taking ownership of your actions and behaviors—and leads you to blaming others, even God, for your life's outcomes.[58]

Having an external locus of control is directly related to depression.[59]

From my standpoint, this is an unhealthy view of God, assuming God to be some dictator and control freak. From a relational standpoint, it would be impossible to have a healthy relationship where one party governs and dictates everything that happens to the other party. This view makes us God's puppets, where God determines our ultimate destiny. Hence, the impact of this perspective on your Future Self is ultimately destructive, because you have absolutely no say in what your Future Self becomes.

Any view that removes agency toward your Future Self is limiting.

Another common view is that God is the creator and we are God's creations. From this belief system, God created everything including the Earth and us out of nothing. From this view, God is a fundamentally different type of being than we are. God is unknowable and incomprehensible to us. It's widely acknowledged that this view of God stems from Greek philosophy.[60]

The analogy of this perspective could be that God is like the potter and we're like a piece of pottery. To further the analogy, the pot and the potter are completely different, and seemingly unrelated. The pot can never understand the potter. The pot could never aspire to truly connect with the potter, let alone be like the potter.

A limitation of this view is the wedge or an eternal divide it creates between God and humanity. From this perspective, we can never truly comprehend or relate with God. We can worship God and be amazed by God and God's creations, but we can't know why God created us, who God is, or who we are. This perspective leaves us with a confused identity and lack of clear sense for our trajectory.

The final framework I'll share is the one I personally resonate with most, and which I believe to be most truthful and inspiring. In this view, God is the parent of humanity, and every person is God's literal offspring[61] and heir.[62]

From this view, all people lived in the presence of God before coming to Earth, and each person on this planet consciously chose, of their own volition, to have this mortal experience. This mortal experience is a step up and step forward in our evolution. Life is like a school, incubator, or simulation, purely experiential and developmental.[63] We all chose our own experiences and lessons.

In the book, *If Life Is a Game, These Are the Rules*, Cherie Carter-Scott presents 10 rules for life.[64]

1. You will receive a body.

2. You will receive lessons—you are enrolled in a full-time informal school called "life."

3. There are no mistakes, only lessons.

4. Lessons are repeated until they are learned.

5. Learning lessons does not end—if you're alive, that means there is still lessons to be learned.

6. "There" is no better than "here."

7. Other people are merely mirrors of you—you cannot love or hate something about someone unless it reflects to you something you love or hate about yourself.

8. What you make of life is up to you—you have all the tools and resources you need, what you do with them is up to you.

9. The answers to life's questions lie within you— all you need to do is look, listen, and trust.

10. You will forget all of this at birth.

These 10 rules reflect the words of the 18th-century English Romantic poet William Wordsworth, who penned:

> Our birth is but a sleep and a forgetting:
> The Soul that rises with us, our life's Star, Hath
> had elsewhere its setting,
> And cometh from afar: Not in entire forgetfulness,
> And not in utter nakedness,
> But trailing clouds of glory do we come
> From God, who is our home
> Heaven lies about us in our infancy.

In Wordsworth's words, we came *from* God.
God is our home.

This life is a forgetting of where we came from, why we're here, and where we're going.

But the answers lie within us.

Being a literal child of God means there is a reason for being here. Life isn't random. We came from God and chose to come here for development, education, and experience. Moreover, being a literal child of God means that within us is the inherent capacity to become like God, *in all ways.* Just as a baby chick doesn't grow up to become a cow, if we are the children of God, then our natural evolution is to become as God is.

Some people worry that this viewpoint is dangerous because it brings God to the level of humanity. If we are the literal offspring of God, then what is God? The 19th-century religious teacher Lorenzo Snow stated, "As man now is, God once was; as God now is, man may be."

Like a parent to a child, or an acorn to an oak, God is a more developed version of us. If we saw God, we would see an advanced person; hence, we were "created in the image of God."[65] This perspective of God as our parent, unlike any other view I've encountered both elevates humanity and unites us with God. We came from God, and are God's children with divine, limitless potential. To quote the 19th-century poet and writer Eliza Snow:

In the heav'ns are parents single?

No, the thought makes reason stare!

Truth is reason; truth eternal

Tells me I've a mother there.

When I leave this frail existence,

When I lay this mortal by,

Father, Mother, may I meet you

In your royal courts on high?[66]

With the innate capacity to become like God in all ways, what does that say about your Future Self? It means that whatever God is, you can become and have all of that. *All of it.*

Wordsworth's and Snow's perspective aren't new or unique. The philosophical term for this view of God is known as *theosis* or deification, which means to "make divine."[67,68,69] We see the theosis perspective as early as the second century. For instance, Irenaeus, a Greek bishop who lived from 115–202 A.D., stated:

> We have not been made gods from the beginning, but at first merely men, then at length gods . . . Passing beyond the angels, and be made after the image and likeness of God.[70,71]

The famous 20th-century writer and theologian C. S. Lewis was an ardent believer and advocate of the theosis perspective of God and humanity. As he said:

> It is a serious thing to live in a society of possible gods and goddesses, to remember that the dullest and most uninteresting person you talk to may one day be a creature which you would be strongly tempted to worship . . . There are no ordinary people.[72]

To me, this is the most intuitive, persuasive, and powerful view of both God and humanity.

I also love the words of Lewis, that, "There are no ordinary people." This view of God enables me to look at every person with awe and amazement.

Every person has the inherent capacity to become like God. This life is a small step in our evolution. Infinity extends behind us and infinity stretches before us. A person's trajectory is far more powerful and real than their current self.

Inherent in this perspective is the belief that we chose to engage in this earthly experience as an important step in our own evolution. We saw our Future Selves in this experience. If we continue evolving, it will be because we choose to do so. Although the children of God, God gives us the freedom to decide what and who we become. There is no force or coercion. To quote the 1805 hymn, first published by Elias Smith and Abner Jones, the original author is unknown:

> Know this, that ev'ry soul is free
>
> To choose his life and what he'll be;
>
> For this eternal truth is giv'n:
>
> That God will force no man to heav'n.
>
> He'll call, persuade, direct aright,
>
> And bless with wisdom, love, and light,
>
> In nameless ways be good and kind,
>
> But never force the human mind.[73]

God loves and respects us irrespective of what we choose.

Truth #7 is that your view of God impacts your Future Self. Your perceived destiny and identity are inseparable.

Each person should be fully respected in what they choose to believe about God, about life, and about themselves. We are all extremely ignorant and limited in our current perspectives, and our Future Selves will see things from a more elevated state.

CONCLUSION

FUTURE SELF TRUTHS

Your Future Self is the driver of your life.

Your Future Self is different than you expect.

Your Future Self is inevitable, yet the outcome is optional.

Your Future Self is what you're measuring.

Failing as your Future Self is how you succeed.

Being successful is only possible by being true to your Future Self.

Your view of God impacts your views of your own Future Self.

In this section of the book, we've covered the seven core truths about your Future Self. These truths, if understood, will enable you to realize a much bolder and more powerful Future Self. You'll be freed from the fixed mindset of being stuck as your current self.

Next, we dive into the seven steps to be your Future Self now. As you apply these steps, you'll be able to clarify and prioritize your Future Self, and eliminate anything less.

Step #1:   Clarify your contextual purpose

Step #2:   Eliminate lesser goals

Step #3:   Elevate from needing to wanting to knowing

Step #4:   Ask for exactly what you want

Step #5:   Automate and systemize your Future Self

Step #6:   Schedule your Future Self

Step #7:   Aggressively complete imperfect work

PART 3

7 STEPS FOR BEING YOUR FUTURE SELF

"Simple can be harder than complex: You have to work hard to get your thinking clean to make it simple. But it's worth it in the end because once you get there, you can move mountains."

—Steve Jobs[1]

When Steve Jobs returned to Apple in 1997, the company teetered on the brink of failure.

During the final quarter of 1996, Apple's sales plummeted by 30 percent. The stock dipped to a 12-year low while Microsoft rose as the dominant computer company in the market.

Jobs felt overwhelmed by the sheer number of confusing products Apple produced, including the same product in dozens of versions.

"Which ones," Jobs wanted to know, "do I tell my friends to buy?"

When management couldn't provide a simple answer, Jobs immediately cut their catalog by 70 percent and downsized the company from approximately 8,000 employees to 5,000.

"Deciding what not to do is as important as deciding what to do," Jobs said. "It's true for companies, and it's true for products."[2]

Moving forward, Apple produced only four products.

For professionals, Apple created the Power Macintosh G3 desktop and the PowerBook G3 portable computer. For consumers, there was the iMac desktop and the iBook portable computer.

Jobs's strategy was simple: focus on fewer products and dramatically improve the quality and innovation of the few.

During Jobs's first fiscal year back at the helm, Apple operated a mere 90 days from being insolvent and more than $1 billion in the red. Yet, through Jobs's strategy of eliminating distracting products and laser focusing on the essentials, Apple turned a $309 million profit during his second year back.

Jobs's master plan had always been to impact the entire *world*. That was even the term he used in 1983 to recruit

John Sculley, a leader at Pepsi. "Do you want to sell sugar water for the rest of your life, or do you want to come with me and change the world?"

By bringing the Apple team together, and helping them create a select few world-changing concepts, Jobs laid the groundwork for Apple's continued innovation. The company introduced revolutionary products including the iPod in 2001, Apple iTunes Store in 2003, the iPhone in 2007, and the iPad in 2010.

Jobs himself was a complex genius that no biographer or psychologist will ever fully understand, but his strategy for success was simple. Jobs held a definite attitude about how the future should be, and courageously fought for his convictions. He was an essentialist who focused on "less, but better," quality over quantity.[3]

Early in his career, Jobs was extremely rough around the edges and lacked leadership skills. This combination led to getting fired from his own company. During his 11 years away from Apple, he learned humility and leadership, and the skills to innovate and change the world.

During his exile years, Jobs invested in Pixar Studios, and helped them with their first major film, *Toy Story*. That movie made him a billionaire before he returned to Apple.

When he came back, he wasn't the same guy.

Yes, he still had his genius and zeal.

He still had a similar overarching vision.

But his brash former self had been tempered with experience and wisdom. Despite disappointments and setbacks, his commitment to a Future Self who would change the world led him to turn a near bankrupt company into the most valuable company on the planet.

Jobs's story provides a solid foundation for the seven core steps to being your desired Future Self. As with all learning, the process can feel messy and some moments will be dark.

Your Future Self will guide you.

Your Future Self will be compassionate toward your mistakes along the way. Certainly, they have a far more elevated and wiser perspective than you and I have now.

With the threats and truths behind you, you're ready for the concrete steps to be your Future Self now.

There's no more time to wait.

Your Future Self is ready for you.

STEP #1

CLARIFY YOUR CONTEXTUAL PURPOSE

"The height of sophistication is simplicity."

–Clare Boothe Luce[4]

As a prisoner in the concentration camps, Victor Frankl helped fellow inmates maintain sanity and hope by, "giving [them] inner strength by pointing out to [them] a future goal to which [they] could look forward."[5]

Frankl wasn't trying to help the prisoners discover some overarching life's purpose. Instead, he wanted to help them clarify a specific goal or purpose for their lives then and there. They needed a contextual purpose for where they were at that particular moment.

For Frankl, surviving the camps meant he could reconstruct his book *The Doctor and the Soul*.

That was his purpose. That highly specific future goal gave meaning to his life and enabled him to bear his sufferings. His Future Self gave him the power to survive.

Once released from the camps, with *The Doctor and the Soul* published, Frankl's purpose shifted to something else that gave his life meaning and direction.

People often become blocked when it comes to envisioning their future. It's common to attempt discovering grand purpose for one's entire life. After all, then you'll be who you really are, and life will be easy and make sense.

Yes, it's nice to have clarity about what you ultimately want for yourself and for your life. But it's also crucial to be open to your values, perspectives, and situation changing. Your Future Self will see things differently than you do now. In a few years, your Future Self will have a different perspective, and likely have different goals than you have now.

Rather than attempting to define your life's purpose, follow Frankl's wisdom. Define for yourself a contextual purpose that you believe to be the absolute most important thing you could do *right now*.

This purpose shouldn't be beyond 10 years out.

Even five years away may be a stretch.

For Jobs, his overarching purpose was to change the world. But for a time, his contextual purpose was to specifically create and launch the iPod. Once he completed that focused and deliberate purpose, he moved to his next contextual purpose.

Given your current context, what is the absolute most important thing you could achieve or realize right now?

What is the next level that would be utterly amazing to achieve?

Step #1: Clarifying your contextual purpose involves three key items:

1. Connect with your long-term Future Self

2. Clarify your contextual purpose through your three major priorities

3. Set massive 12-month targets based on your three priorities

Connecting with your long-term Future Self is essential to quality decisions in the present. The further out you imagine and connect, the more informed and strategic you can be. Of course, your Future Self will adapt and change, but that does not discount the importance of being connected.

After connecting to your long-term Future Self, the next step is to clarify the most important objective you could accomplish now. This is your contextual purpose.

You define your contextual purpose through a refined set of objectives. These priorities are what you believe are absolutely most important to you and your Future Self.

The challenge most people face is that they don't have clear priorities.

In the iconic business book *Good to Great*, Jim Collins explained the differences between most good companies and the few that become insanely successful. Collins found the majority of companies and individuals simply have way too many goals. They're unfocused and spread thin.

Companies that succeed at the absolute highest level have no more than three core objectives they're trying to accomplish. As Collins stated:

> If you have more than three priorities, you don't have any.[6]

Having too many competing goals or objectives is the major problem we all face.

Like Collins, Gino Wickman found this to be true among his entrepreneurial clients. Wickman is the creator of the Entrepreneurial Operating System (EOS) used by

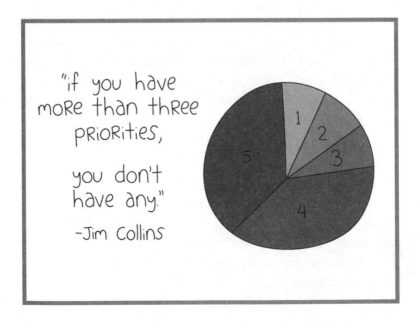

"if you have more than three priorities,

you don't have any."

—Jim Collins

tens of thousands of successful entrepreneurs worldwide. Wickman helps entrepreneurs clarify what they're doing, simplify their processes and goals, and ultimately get massive traction.

As he stated in his book *Traction*:

> Most companies make the mistake of trying to accomplish too many objectives per year. By trying to get everything done all at once, they end up accomplishing very little and feeling frustrated. One client of mine was stubborn on this point for the first few years . . . Each year we set goals, he would keep piling on more. When we were done, the company would have 12 to 15 goals for the year. Like clockwork, at the end of the year, they would accomplish very little and end up frustrated. Going into the third year, he finally had a revelation: They were taking on too much. With this awareness, we agreed that the team could choose only three goals for the coming year. They did, and by the end of the year, they accomplished all three, increased sales by 19 percent, and had their most profitable year in five years.

Your life is like a garden. If you're not intentional, your garden will be overrun with weeds and randomness. This occurs if you have too many competing goals and priorities.

Growing your Future Self requires investing in your Future Self. Investing in your Future Self is akin to planting and nourishing seeds that eventually bear fruit. To determine which seeds to plant, first determine which fruit or outcomes you want for your Future Self.

If you want to eat salsa in your future, focus your garden on tomatoes, peppers, onions, and cilantro. Skip the sweet potatoes.

It's key to ask: *What are you optimizing for?*

Who do you want your Future Self to be?

What few areas do you want to prioritize and invest big in so you can create 10X compounding results? What seeds or investments do you want to plant that will yield the greatest return?

For instance, if you really want your Future Self to be far healthier, then wellness is an area of focus and major investment. If you want your Future Self to have an abundance of passive-income generating assets, then finance is a core priority.

Only you can decide what you want to optimize for your Future Self.

Only you can determine what specific seeds to plant, and what you want your life to look like.

The second key to clarify your Future Self is defining your purpose with three clear priorities.

What three priorities, if realized, would take your life to a totally different level? These are the three areas of focus you want to dramatically invest in to create 10X compounding results. These priorities are the most important areas of focus at this particular point in time. In the future, you will likely have different priorities.

As a teenager, my single purpose was to get on a church mission following high school. I had no idea what my life held after that mission. But I believed that getting on that mission was the absolute most important thing I could do for my Future Self.

Not go to college.

Not figure out what I would do with my life.

Not begin my career.

Just go on that mission.

If I could get to that mile marker, I'd figure out what to do next from there.

That purpose probably saved my life, just as Frankl's purpose saved his. During my teen years, I experienced a lot of trauma and confusion. My parents had gone through a brutal divorce, my father battled an extreme drug addiction, and there wasn't much stability in my home.

Without that North Star of serving a mission, I would likely have sunk into the chaos around me. I knew that to serve a mission, I needed a high school diploma. With the mission as my goal, I barely graduated high school, but I graduated. I needed to uphold various standards to become a missionary, which enabled me to not get lost in the drugs and similar traps around me.

Once I got home from that mission in 2010 at age 22, my contextual purpose for the next five years was three fold:

1. Get married

2. Finish college

3. Get into a Ph.D. program

Despite zero college experience and zero college credits to my name, I knew I wanted to attend Brigham Young University. BYU is just about as competitive and difficult to get into as some Ivy League universities. But my objective remained clear. I earned straight A's at Salt Lake Community College and was accepted to BYU.

I met Lauren during my second semester and we were married eight months later. My first attempt applying to

Ph.D. programs met with rejection from 15 different schools. Getting rejected turned out to be a major gain, because that led me to find perhaps the best mentor I've ever had, Dr. Nate Lambert. Together, Nate and I wrote and submitted nearly 20 papers for publication. With this experience, I applied to universities I wanted to attend, and eventually chose to pursue a Ph.D. in organizational psychology at Clemson University.

Upon entering my Ph.D. program in 2014, my contextual purpose for the next five years was threefold:

1. Grow our family

2. Finish my Ph.D.

3. Begin my writing career and become a professional writer

Shortly after getting to Clemson, Lauren and I became the foster parents of three children. We spent the next three years battling the foster system until February of 2018 when we were miraculously granted adoption. One month after the adoption, after years of fertility treatments, Lauren became pregnant with twin girls via in vitro fertilization (IVF). Our twins were born December of 2018.

In early 2015, during my second semester at Clemson, I started blogging online. Over the next two years, I wrote hundreds of blog posts and grew a sizable email list. In January of 2017, I landed my first book deal, and in March of 2018, *Willpower Doesn't Work* was published. In 2019, I finished my Ph.D. and signed book deals for my next two books, *Personality Isn't Permanent* and *Who Not How*, both of which were published in 2020.

That brings me to the present moment. Lauren and I now have six children, our last child, Rex, was born in

November of 2020. We live in Orlando and our three older kids are 14, 12, and 10.

Given our stage in life, our purpose and priorities are different from what they were five years ago when we were first starting out at Clemson.

We're not the same people we were.

We're not in the same situation.

We don't have the same contextual purpose.

In a recent conversation, Lauren and I discussed what would be the most important areas of focus for us over the next few years. We decided that our top priority is our older three kids since they are making their way through their teen years and will launch into being adults soon.

As of 2021, my contextual purpose for the next five years is threefold:

1. **Family**—with a massive emphasis on my three older kids

2. **Books**—10Xing my career as an author in terms of quality of books published and number of books sold

3. **Finances**—10Xing my net worth and securing my long-term finances for myself and my family

These are the areas I want to optimize for my Future Self. This is the fruit I want my Future Self to experience. These are the areas I'm going to make massive and focused investments in to assure these specific areas grow and compound massively.

I shared my priorities simply to give an example. The specifics of my current priorities and focus are not what matters.

The question for you to answer is: *What is your current purpose?*

Who is your Future Self at your next level?

Can you give your Future Self context and make your vision vivid, detailed, and personal to you?

What three priorities of focus are absolutely most crucial and essential for you right now? Do your three priorities embody the purpose you feel is most important for you to fulfill? Do these three priorities resonate deeply and excite you?

For additional training and resources, including the *3 Priorities Checklist*, go to futureself.com.

After you clarify and define your core three priorities, set specific and measurable 12-month goals for each one. Here are my own 2022 goals:

1. **FAMILY**
   a. Take 150 free non-work days during 2022 (Wednesdays, Saturdays, Sundays), where I invest in my family and have peak experiences
   b. Six-week summer Europe trip
   c. Monthly one-on-one with the older kids
   d. Huge focus and investment in their sports and other interests

2. **BOOKS**
   a. Publish *Be Your Future Self Now* and *10X Is Easier Than 2X*
   b. Sell more than 1,000,000 books between all of my published works
   c. Determine my next collaboration for a 2023 book

3. **FINANCES**
   a. Reach my financial freedom target, the amount of assets that would enable me to live well off the growing equity

Once you've clarified your three core priorities, set specific goals for each of those priorities over the next 12 months.

Rank in order those goals in terms of which are the absolute most important. Which of your 12-month goals, if achieved, would make the biggest long-term impact for your Future Self?

Rank-ordering my top three goals for 2022:

1. 150 free days with family for connection, recovery, presence, slowing time down

2. Publish two books

3. Reach financial freedom target

Once you've rank-ordered your top three 12-month goals, ask yourself which of these could I potentially 10X in the next 12 months?

The goal determines the process.

A fundamental aspect of hope is pathways thinking. When you 10X any of your goals, you'll have to really reconsider your current process or pathway.

As Dan Sullivan said, "When 10X is your measuring stick, you immediately see how you can bypass what everyone else is doing." For example, if I 10X my financial goal for 2022, I'd have to totally rethink my current plan and process. Obviously, my current approach and game plan wouldn't get me to 10X. Thus, if I'm serious about 10Xing a certain area, I need to find or create a much more powerful and direct path. This occurs through trial and error. My Future Self, even next week, knows way more than I do this week. 10X requires focus and simplicity.

Which one of your 12-month goals is most ripe for a 10X jump?

Step #1 to being your Future Self is to clarify your contextual purpose. By clarifying and contextualizing your Future Self, you move to Step #2, which is removing everything that conflicts with the purpose and priorities you've created.

STEP #2

ELIMINATE LESSER GOALS

*"We are kept from our goal not by obstacles,
but by a clear path to a lesser goal."*

—Robert Brault

In 1975, a young boy in England, known for devouring comics and carrying a book everywhere, wrote a list of things his Future Self would accomplish: "Write an adult novel, a children's book, a comic, a movie, record an audiobook, write an episode of *Doctor Who* . . . "

As Neil Gaiman grew older, his list evolved. He wanted to be "an author, primarily of fiction, making good books, making good comics and supporting myself through my words."

A strategy he used for reaching his goals was imagining his Future Self as a distant mountain he walked toward. Every time he was presented an opportunity, he asked himself, "Does this take me closer to or further from the mountain?"

If a particular opportunity did not take him closer to the mountain, Neil said, "No."

As he stated in a commencement speech in 2012:

> I knew that as long as I kept walking towards the mountain, I would be all right. And when I truly was not sure what to do, I could stop, and think about whether it was taking me towards or away from the mountain. I said no to editorial jobs on magazines, proper jobs that would have paid proper money because I knew, that attractive though they were, for me they would have been walking away from the mountain. And if those job offers had come along earlier, I might have taken them, because they still would have been closer to the mountain than I was at the time.

Neil's mountain strategy worked. He became one of the world's most famous fiction authors and a pioneer of adult comics. His books have won awards including the Hugo, Nebula, and Bram Stoker, as well as the Newbery and Carnegie medals.

With his pervious mountains far behind him, Neil became his desired Future Self and more. His Future Self continues to evolve. He arrived at his mountain by staying focused and eliminating conflicting and lesser goals along the way.

Your results follow what you're most committed to in a single instant. The easiest way to see what you're committed to is by observing your own behavior. If you're trying to work on a project, but continually distract yourself with other things, then you're committed to the distractions. The distractions are the greater goal in that moment.

If you say you're committed to having an amazing retirement, but consistently spend away your paycheck, then you're committed to spending, not investing.

If you say you're committed to starting a side hustle, but your spare time is spent on social media or with friends, then you're committed to social media and friends, not your side hustle.

When Neil said, "no" to the editorial jobs, he proved his commitment to the mountain.

Your behavior reflects what you see as your Future Self. Your behavior reflects your commitment, and therefore, your results reflect your commitment.

To re-quote Jim Dethmer, Diana Chapman, and Kaley Klemp:

> Commitment is a statement of what "is." You can know what you're committed to by your results, not by what you say your commitments are. We are all

committed. We are all producing results. The result is proof of a commitment.[7]

Right now, you're committed to your current life and habits. You're committed to your current results. You're reading this book because you want better results. You want new commitments.

Once you've clarified a specific goal, you have to ask yourself: *Am I committed enough to uncommit to what I currently have?*

If you truly are committed to something new and better, you'll stop much of what you're currently doing.

Step #2 of being your Future Self is simplifying your life by removing lesser goals. In every moment, you're faced with one of two options: Commit to your mountain or yield to a lesser goal.

That lesser goal could be an infinite number of things from checking email or social media to eating that dessert. It could be continuing your day job when you know you want something different.

Anything that isn't taking you toward your Future Self is a lesser goal.

About commitment, the late Harvard business professor Clayton Christensen said, "100 percent is easier than 98 percent." It's easier to commit to something 100 percent, because once you've committed, you've eliminated the internal conflict. You've silenced the decision fatigue. You've banished the lesser goals.

Commitment requires vigilance. There's never a time when lesser goals won't present themselves to you.

Often, we maintain many of our habits or relationships because we're scared to commit. We're frightened of the repercussions of that commitment. So rather than eliminate our clear paths to lesser goals, we continue to maintain the lesser paths.

Motivationally, our goal-conflicting behavior makes sense. To have motivation, you have a compelling outcome or reward, a path for attaining that outcome, and the confidence to execute that path.[8] Lesser goals are compelling because they're easy. They offer a quick reward or dopamine hit. Probably, we commit to our lesser goals far more than we commit to our genuine wishes.

Lesser goals are weeds in the garden of life. Every time you engage in a lesser goal, it's the equivalent of planting a weed in your garden. Whatever you plant will produce your results.

What is your garden producing? Is your garden optimized for your Future Self? Or is it totally chaotic and full of weeds?

In Step #1, we clarified your contextual purpose. We defined your core three priorities. We set specific and measurable targets for each priority. We shaped your mountain. We visualized your garden.

This is the Future Self you want, right?

This is your purpose, which according to Viktor Frankl, gives your life meaning.

To realize your Future Self, commit 100 percent to your purpose. Your purpose and identity are interconnected. Your identity is what you're most committed to. Your identity follows your purpose.

If you're going to realize your purpose, then Step #2 to being your Future Self is uncommitting to lesser goals. These lesser goals are structural aspects of your current life, and the moment-by-moment decisions you make throughout your day.

By structural aspects, I mean your current habits, behaviors, and relationships. There are a lot of things you do throughout your day that conflict with your contextual purpose.

What are those lesser goals?

What are the major things in your life that oppose your contextual purpose?

What in your life is outside your three priorities?

What are you still saying "yes" to that your desired Future Self would say "no" to?

What are you continuing to commit to and invest in that is taking you away from where you want to go?

This assessment requires brutal honesty.

Your behavior clearly reflects, in every moment, what you're committed to. In every instant, you're presented with the option to live your purpose or submit to some lesser goal.

Eliminating lesser goals is a continual process. As a writer, every day and every moment, I have the choice: write the book or do something else. Life is dynamic, not static. In almost every instance, you have multiple options, distractions, other people's agendas, and your own conflicting desires. It takes mindfulness and discernment to know, in a given moment, what is the best decision to make.

For instance, if your child has an injury, or in the case of an emergency, clearly you need to head to the hospital. But in most moments, the path may not be that obvious, unless, like Gaiman, we have a specific mountain to move toward.

Only after you've committed to a specific purpose with clear priorities can you discern what's best to do in a given moment.

Is this taking me toward my objective?

Is this the most effective thing I can do? If the answer is "No," then refocus on your vision. When you slip and pursue a lesser goal, quickly recommit to your vision.

The French writer and poet Antoine de Saint-Exupéry said,

> Perfection is achieved, not when there is nothing more to add, but when there is nothing left to take away.

perfection is not when
there's nothing left to add

"●"

perfection is when there's
nothing left to Remove

What lesser goals can you immediately eliminate?

Each day, and in each moment, you'll face goal conflicts. What will you do as those moments arise?

Your behavior demonstrates what you're truly committed to.

Step #2 of being your Future Self is removing lesser goals. This is a fundamental step of being your Future Self now.

ELEVATE FROM NEEDING TO WANTING TO KNOWING

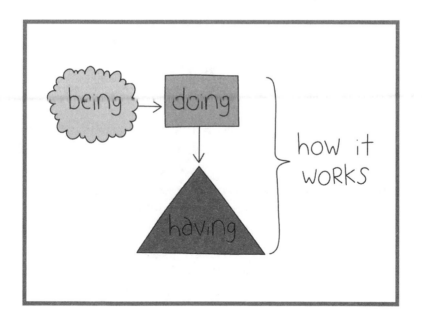

"Do or not do. There is no try."

–Yoda

Dr. David Hawkins created what is known as the *map of consciousness*.[9] This map reflects levels of emotional development ranging from the lower levels of shame, fear, and anger to the higher levels of courage, acceptance, love, and enlightenment.

The higher you progress on Hawkins's map, the easier it is to create the life you want. The lower you are on the map, the more friction, resistance, and pain will be in your life. Progressing through the levels is the process of evolving from needing to wanting to knowing.

When you think you need something, you have an unhealthy attachment to it. Needing implies you are in a deep state of lack and can't be whole or happy until the need is filled.

Wanting is healthier than needing, but wanting is still a state of lack. To want assumes you don't possess what you want.

Knowing is a higher level than wanting. Knowing is the acceptance that you already have what you want. You can live in a state of acceptance, peace, and gratitude. As Florence Shinn, the early 20th-century writer and mystic, said, "Faith knows it has already received and acts according."[10]

In similar fashion, the actor Denzel Washington stated, "True desire, in the heart, for anything good is God's proof to you sent beforehand to indicate that it's yours already."

When you know something is yours, you act differently than if you don't know. A salesperson who knows they are going to make a sale behaves differently than the salesperson who wants to make a sale.

If a person knows they're going to get up the next morning and go to the gym, they'll be different from the person who simply wants to. Knowing is an inner experience, a state of acceptance.

Close your eyes and imagine your Future Self in specific detail. Imagine yourself where you want to be. Are you living in a particular home? Cozy by the fireplace with your lover? Are you completing a marathon at a certain pace?

Accept the vision as something you know you already have. Inhale acceptance. If you want, pray and ask God if you can have this, and wait for peace to rest upon your soul. Feel that peace and smile. Genuinely express gratitude for your vision.

Author and teacher Dr. Joe Dispenza stated:

> Gratitude is a powerful emotion to use for manifesting because normally we feel gratitude *after* we receive something. So, the emotional signature of gratitude means it has already happened. When you are thankful or you feel appreciation, you are in the ultimate state to receive. When you embrace gratitude, your body, as the unconscious mind, will begin to believe it is in a future reality in the present moment. You have to really feel the emotions of your future. This is not an intellectual process—it is a visceral one. What do you believe you're worthy to receive? Can you teach your body emotionally what it will feel like to receive what it is you want before it happens? In order for it to manifest you have to be able to do this in the present moment.

A primary reason people don't get what they want is because they don't feel worthy to have it. They can visualize their desired goal mentally, but emotionally resist owning the reality.

They don't believe their Future Self.

They don't feel abundance can be theirs.

They're blocked, and resist.

Napoleon Hill stated, "Whatever the mind can conceive *and believe*, the mind can achieve." He further stated, "If you make your prayers an expression of gratitude and thanksgiving for the blessings you already have, instead of requests for things you do not have, you will obtain results much faster."[11]

Gratitude is powerful when expressed for what has already occurred. It's also extremely powerful when you express proactive gratitude for what you want in the future. Gratitude elevates from wanting to knowing.

When I truly want something, I meditate, visualize the desire as already mine, and pray until I reach a state of knowing. For example, while closing my eyes and seeing the house I want my family to live in, I deeply inhale acceptance of having this home and softy exhale gratitude for the reality to be. I totally accept that what I want is already mine.

I'm at total peace.

There's no lack. Only utter gratitude and acceptance.

In the classic book *As A Man Thinketh*, James Allen, wrote, "Men do not attract that which they want, but that which they are."[12]

This is why getting to a place of knowing and acceptance is crucial. This is why you must be your Future Self now.

Your behavior follows your identity. The scientific definition of *identity* is "a well-organized conception of the self, consisting of values and beliefs to which the individual is solidly committed."[13]

Your identity is what you're most committed to.

As you align your identity with your Future Self, fully accepting the truth of it, then you act *as* your Future Self. Dr. Stephen Covey said, "To know and not to do is really not to know."[14]

When you know, you will do.

To know and not do is to not know.

To repeat Florence Shinn, "Faith *knows* it has already received and *acts* accordingly." Faith is knowing. That knowing automatically leads to an elevated and aligned doing.

Every little action you take toward your Future Self enhances your level of commitment and knowing. Every little action toward your Future Self is the evidence of your faith.

Every little action toward your Future Self is you more fully being your Future Self now.

"to know and not do is really not to know."

-DR. Stephen R. Covey

Knowing and being in advance are key to having. Zig Ziglar stated, "You have to *be* before you can *do*, and *do* before you can *have*." This is the reverse of how most people approach their desires, and why few people live the life they want. The common approach is to believe you must have something first, which will enable you to do and ultimately be what you want.

For example, say you want to be an entrepreneur. You might think you first need to have funding, or a brilliant idea, or [fill in the blank], which will enable you to do what you want to do and ultimately be who you want to be.

Believing you must first have something leads people down endless paths of lesser goals that never lead them where they want to go. As an example, I have a friend who would love to retire and do full-time humanitarian service. But he believes he must first have certain credentials, finances, and experiences. Rather than being his Future Self now, he spends decades accumulating qualifiers that he believes will enable him to eventually do and be what he wants.

What he doesn't realize is that he could be his Future Self now. If he started with being, which is knowing, then his doing would come *from* his Future Self, rather than from his current and limited self.

Accept and know that what you want is yours, and you can be and do *from* your goal, rather than *to* your goal. You know you've already succeeded, and act *from* the position and mindset of your Future Self. Because you're acting *from* the goal, rather than toward the goal, your actions are far more powerful and aligned.

Your actions come from your identity. When your identity is rooted in current commitments, rather than your Future Self, your actions are weak and unaligned with your goal. The only way to realize your Future Self is to *be* your Future Self now.

Be, then do, then have.

Once you accept the truth of your Future Self, and know it's already yours, then your actions align with your vision. Your circumstances change immediately. You see what you didn't previously see. You stop doing what no longer aligns.

This takes us to Step #4, where in a state of knowing, you directly ask for exactly what you want. You'll see paths and relationships that will get you to your goals. As William Hutchinson Murray put it:

> Until one is committed, there is hesitancy, the chance to draw back, always ineffectiveness. Concerning all acts of initiative (and creation), there is one elementary truth, the ignorance of which kills countless ideas and splendid plans: that the moment one definitely commits oneself, then Providence moves too. All sorts of things occur to help one that would never otherwise have occurred. A whole stream of events issues from the decision, raising in one's favor all manner of unforeseen incidents and meetings and material assistance, which no man could have dreamt would have come his way.

STEP #4

ASK FOR EXACTLY WHAT YOU WANT

ask and
you shall
Receive

*"Ask, and it shall be given you . . .
For every one that asketh receiveth."*

–Matthew 7:7-8, King James Bible

For the five years immediately following college, Amanda Palmer spent her days as a living statue. She painted her skin white, wore a white dress, and stood on a crate in a public square with an upturned hat at her feet.

When someone threw in a dollar, she made eye contact and handed them a white flower.

At night, Palmer played local shows as the pianist and lyricist in her duo, the Dresden Dolls. As her music grew popular, she made enough money to quit her statue job. Yet, as the Dresden Dolls toured, she didn't want to lose that direct human contact she felt making eye contact with strangers on the streets.

After shows, the band signed autographs and took pictures with fans. They made an art of asking their fans to help them, mostly using Twitter. As Palmer stated in her TED Talk, *The Art of Asking*:

> So, I would need a piano to practice on, and an hour later I would be at a fan's house. People would bring home-cooked food to us all over the world backstage and feed us and eat with us. Fans who worked in museums and stores and any kind of public space would wave their hands if I would decide to do a last-minute, spontaneous, free gig. I once tweeted, "Where in Melbourne can I buy a neti pot?" And a nurse from a hospital drove one right at that moment to the cafe I was in, and I bought her a smoothie and we sat there talking about nursing and death.

But then, Palmer's asking became far different from just asking for random favors. As the Dresden Dolls' popularity continued to grow, they were offered a deal with a major record label. They signed the contract and released an album that sold 25,000 copies. The label considered the release a failure.

One night after a show, Palmer signed autographs and hugged fans. A guy approached and handed her a $10 bill. "I'm sorry, I burned your CD from a friend. But I read your blog, I know you hate your label. I just want you to have this money."

People continued to hand Palmer money for her music. But unlike working with the middleman, Palmer had direct contact with those giving her funds. She decided from then on to give her music away for free. She also decided that whenever she needed help, she'd ask directly.

She left her record label and for her next project with her new band, Grand Theft Orchestra, she turned to crowdfunding.

> The goal was 100,000 dollars. My fans backed me at nearly 1.2 million, which was the biggest music crowdfunding project to date. And you can see how many people it is. It's about 25,000 people.

Palmer recommends we ask without shame. We learn to trust, and to give and receive. She ends her TED Talk by saying:

> I think people have been obsessed with the wrong question, which is, "How do we make people pay for music?" What if we started asking, "How do we let people pay for music?"

Everything Palmer has in her life she gets by asking.

Graham Stephen is a YouTuber with millions of subscribers who talks about finance. At the beginning of every video, he finds clever ways to ask his audience to like his video and subscribe to his channel. Sometimes, he spends 30–60 seconds asking for likes and subscribes. He's gotten so entertaining that his fans aren't put off, but laugh with him.

Of course, some people criticize Graham for being so forthright. "If your videos are good, you shouldn't need to ask for likes and subscribes."

And that's where they are wrong.

The reason Graham's channel is successful is largely because he asks his audience to help. Every time someone likes one of his videos, the like adjusts the YouTube algorithm in his favor, placing his videos in front of more people.

In Graham's older videos, he wasn't as direct and shameless about asking for likes and subscribes. Sometimes, he didn't ask at all. Or, if he did, he sounded timid and guilty. But over time, he committed to growing his channel. He stopped being afraid to succeed. He accepted his Future Self, and asked for exactly what he wanted. And because he asked directly for what he wanted, his channel is on fire and he makes millions of dollars.

In his book *The Powers of Two*, Joshua Wolf Shenk said, "When you speak of what you want, and even one person hears, it may begin a generative loop."[15]

The early 19th-century American religious leader and prophet Joseph Smith stated, "Weary the Lord until he blesses you."[16] Joseph was known for giving everything he had, often the shirt off his back. There were times when his own cupboard was bare.

One day his family had nothing to eat but a little cornmeal. They made from the cornmeal what they called a johnnycake, similar to a pancake. Joseph offered this blessing: "Lord, we thank thee for this johnnycake and ask thee to send us something better. Amen."

Before the meal was over, there came a knock at the door. A man brought a ham and flour. In excitement, Joseph jumped to his feet and said to his wife, Emma, "I knew the Lord would answer my prayer."[17,18]

You can know you're committed to something when you ask for it. When you ask directly, boldly, and without apology.

Start asking, and you'll start receiving. It's startling how fast you'll get what you want once you directly ask.

For example, in the past three days, I've opened emails from people offering exactly what I want. There are two things I'm looking for at this particular moment. One is a right-fit collaboration with someone I can write a future book with. I've told others about my goal, knowing it will come. I've received messages from really interesting people, all of whom I would be happy to work with. Additionally, all of whom are happy to pay what I'm asking.

When you ask, the doors open.

Often, we're afraid to ask for exactly what we want because we don't think we can get it. So, we lower what we ask for, and receive at the level of our internal acceptance.

The other thing I'm looking for right now is a ghostwriter to help with the first draft of my next book. This will help me achieve my goals while living out my big three priorities where I focus more on my family. I've been telling people I want a ghostwriter, and just this morning, I got an email from someone who's worked on 30 books, and who also has been a fan of my work for years.

It's almost too easy. You can be the bee who goes out looking for the flowers, or you can be the flower and have the bees come to you.

When you ask directly and clearly for exactly what you want, what you want will come to you. I'm really glad I asked Lauren to go on that first date. I'm glad I kept asking, even when, for a while, she was not interested.

I kept asking, and we finally had a real date.

Then I asked her to marry me.

I remember asking Nate Lambert to be my mentor, and to help him with his papers. I asked Bob Sinclair at Clemson to let me into the Ph.D. program, even though I missed the deadline.

I asked Dan Sullivan if I could write books with him, and we're now working on our third.

Once, while at an academic conference in San Antonio, I worked out in the hotel gym at the same time that several members of the Golden State Warriors were there working out. I asked if they could get me tickets. That night, my professor and I had amazing seats at the game.

You get in life what you ask for. Sometimes, you've got to be persistent in your asking.

And as you evolve, you'll want better things. You'll hone your clarity about your Future Self. And you'll ask for more specific things that better align with your ever-greater Future Self.

Step #4 to being your Future Self is to directly ask for what you want.

Ask God in prayer.

Ask experts.

Ask friends.

Ask anybody.

Just ask. Don't be afraid. And don't be ashamed.

As you get better at clarifying, simplifying, and asking, you'll receive with increased swiftness.

AUTOMATE AND SYSTEMIZE YOUR FUTURE SELF

clarity in the future creates clarity in the here-and-now

"For any challenge, the first thing to do is optimize it. Break it down to its bare minimum, simplify it, and eliminate everything that's not completely necessary . . . After you've optimized a task, the next step is to automate as much as possible. Use software or processes so you can get the task done without human involvement—just set it and forget it. Finally, for anything that's left, outsource to a generalist or a specialist. It's important to note that although outsourcing can do a lot for you, it comes after optimizing and automating. If you outsource an inefficient task, that doesn't really help because it's still inefficient. It's much better to eliminate work by optimizing or automating whenever you can and only outsource what's left."

—Ari Meisel[19]

When I started working with my financial advisor, we discussed my goals and purpose. From there, he suggested I begin auto-investing. Set an amount of money to automatically go from my bank account to my investment account every Monday. Set it and forget it. Over time, increase that amount.

Consistency of investing plus time is what matters most, my advisor explained. Time in the market over timing the market. I set the amount at my comfort level and essentially forgot about it. When I spoke to my advisor three months later, he told me how much my investment account had grown since I started auto-investing.

I was stunned, and motivated. I increased the amount and have regularly increased the amount from time to time.

To get where you want to go faster and easier, automate and systemize your Future Self. Implementing strategic systems frees up your conscious mind to focus, play, and plan. Automation ensures consistency of results.

Business strategist Eben Pagan calls this inevitability thinking, which he defines as, "thinking and acting as if what you are doing is a forgone conclusion because you set up the conditions for it to happen."

Don't be afraid to start small.

Design your system around your Future Self.

System design means you make routines as friction-free and automatic as possible to achieve your goals. Impose friction or barriers where you want to avoid unwanted outcomes. Where can you make one change that creates an ongoing desired effect? For example, removing social media apps from your cell phone makes it easier to avoid mindlessly hopping on and wasting valuable time scrolling.

Designing a system intelligently is possible by first clarifying and simplifying your objectives. As management author and legend Peter Drucker said, "There is nothing quite so useless, as doing with great efficiency, something that should not be done at all."

Effectiveness is doing the right things, while efficiency is doing things right. Effectiveness must always come first, then efficiency. System design is about automating and outsourcing your desired results. Give yourself the space to put your attention and energy where you want. The goal is to off-load your mental and physical plate.

Dan Sullivan and I wrote a book, *Who Not How*. The premise is that if you want to achieve bigger goals, you'll need the right "whos" to take care of most of the hows. If you're trying to do everything yourself, then flow and focus are difficult because there are hundreds of tasks to do.

Getting whos to take care of important tasks is essential to system design. For example, my assistant, Chelsea, serves as the barrier and filter to my mind. I've given her clear criteria for what opportunities I'm interested in, as well as what can go on my schedule. She inbounds dozens of requests weekly for my time, but almost none of those reach my conscious awareness. Once per week, Chelsea and I discuss the opportunities or situations she deems relevant to me.

System design is trial and error, and refinement takes time. In the beginning, Chelsea would bring me opportunities I didn't want, or schedule appointments that ended up frustrating me. But as I've gotten clearer and more committed to my Future Self, we've created a better decision filter for what is relevant.

In this continuous process, patience and practice are key.

In the book *The Paradox of Choice: Why More Is Less*, psychologist Dr. Barry Schwartz explained that having more options leads to decision fatigue and ultimately regretful decisions.[20] Trying to keep too many options available is a lack of intention and commitment. A fundamental aspect of decision-making is gladly accepting opportunity costs.

Once you've clarified and simplified your Future Self, free yourself of decision fatigue, distractions, and all lesser goals. Allow your time and attention to focus on the absolute best and most relevant uses of your time, your three priorities.

Being selectively or strategically ignorant is crucial. It's crucial to become increasingly *unaware* of what's going on in the outside world. As author John Maxwell said, "You cannot overestimate the unimportance of practically everything."[21]

Almost everything in the world outside your "big three" is nonessential. Almost everything is a distraction or lesser goal to your Future Self and your three top priorities.

Little distractions or inputs can infect or alter your entire life. *The Butterfly Effect* is an economic principle explaining that small and imperceptible influences can compound and massively change the overall system.

An example is when wolves were reintroduced to Yellowstone National Park in 1995. For 70 years, the deer population had grown enormously without a predator to hunt them. Humans attempted to control the deer but couldn't. The deer grazed away all the vegetation.

With the small number of wolves introduced, they killed a few deer, but more importantly, the deer avoided certain parts of the park, particularly the valleys and gorges. Immediately, those places regenerated.

In some areas, the height of the trees quintupled. Barren valleys quickly became forests of aspens, willows, and cottonwoods. With the increase in trees, the birds moved in. Beavers increased dramatically, toppling trees to build dams that created habitats for otters, ducks, fish, and reptiles. The number of bears increased because there were abundant berries in the foliage. Because the wolves hunted the coyotes, the mice and rabbit population increased, which nourished hawks, weasels, foxes, and badgers.

Most fascinating, the rivers throughout the Yellowstone became straighter and defined. Channels narrowed and pools formed as the regenerating forests stabilized and strengthened the banks. Wolves changed not only the eco system of Yellowstone, but the physical structure.

Small changes can create nonlinear and non-predictable shifts throughout the system. This is partially why your Future Self will be far different from what you predict. This is also why systems thinking and systems design is so powerful. If you're unaware, you could allow a virus that, initially small, could spread and take over the system. Conversely, you could alter the system, blocking inputs and designing for others to automate and compound the results you want.

Introducing small changes into your system can have a dramatic effect. Refining your system to automate your desired results and block noise and decision fatigue is essential to flow and high performance.

It's crucial to note that even the best system will quickly become outdated. As you evolve and grow, your goals and situation will change. As your vision expands and your commitment to better results increases, you'll improve your system.

Step #5 to being your Future Self is automating and systemizing your Future Self.

How can you better systemize your desired Future Self?

What could you simplify and eliminate from your life, to free yourself from decision fatigue and lesser goals?

What barriers and filters could you create to protect your time and attention?

What could you automate, such as a weekly investing strategy?

Where could you find a who to handle some of the hows that are outside your zone of genius?[22]

STEP #6

Schedule Your Future Self

"To me, 'busy' implies that the person is out of control of their life."

—Derek Sivers[23]

Your schedule reflects your priorities.

Your schedule reflects what you're actually committed to.

Most schedules are dominated by urgent battles and lesser goals such as meetings and Zoom calls. Rarely does someone's schedule reflect and prioritize their Future Self over their current self.

For several years, my schedule was overruled by appointments and meetings, most of which were lesser goals and distractions. They were urgent but not important. I wrote hundreds of blog posts and several books without having book writing in my schedule. While I said writing was my top goal and priority, my calendar proved otherwise since I squeezed that task into the margins.

Step #6 of being your Future Self is scheduling your time around your Future Self. If approached correctly, the principles in Step #6 could 10X or 100X not only your productive output, but more important, enable you to control your own time rather than your schedule controlling you.

In *Who Not How*, Dan Sullivan and I discuss Dan's 4 Freedoms:

1. Freedom of time

2. Freedom of money

3. Freedom of relationship

4. Freedom of purpose[24]

Your time is the clearest indicator of your commitment. You can't hide how you spend your time.

To improve freedom of money, relationships, and purpose, own your Freedom of Time.

To have freedom of time, take ownership of your schedule. Prioritize what matters most, and eliminate what does not. The more you take ownership of your time and attention, the simpler and easier to realize your Future Self. If, however, your time is continually overrun with lesser goals and other people's agendas, then your desired Future Self will be frustrated.

There are two fundamental ways to approach time: Either it's something outside of you that you cannot control, or it's something within you that you fully control. In *The Big Leap*, Dr. Gay Hendricks explains these two models as Newtonian Time versus Einstein Time,

> Einstein time assumes you are where time comes from. You can make as much of it as you want. Newtonian time, assumes there's a scarcity of time, which leads to an uncomfortable feeling of time urgency inside us. And we think that what is "out there" is causing the feelings "in here."[25]

Dr. Joe Dispenza explained, "Newtonian physics is the belief in cause and effect while Einstein physics is the belief of causing the effect. When you're causing the effect, then the quantum field of reality is responding to your thoughts, energy, and actions."

When you realize you are not the effect, but you're the cause of the effects, you multiply ownership over your past, present, and Future Self.

How much ownership are you willing to take of your own time? The more you say "No" to lesser goals, the stronger your commitment grows to creating the life and outcomes you want.

Recently, I've taken these ideas very seriously. To use Covey's term, I decided to "put the big rocks in first." I blocked

Wednesdays, Saturdays, and Sundays as my free days from work. Those three days per week, approximately 150 days per year, are exclusively for family and nonwork activities. *Psychological detachment from work* is a growing concept in occupational psychology that shows the importance of unplugging. If you're always working or always available and never fully recovering, then flow, creativity, and high performance are practically impossible.[26,27]

Two of my primary work goals are to write more and better books, and make lots of YouTube videos. Until recently, I wasn't doing either as successfully as I wanted. I decided to prioritize those goals by assigning them first place in my workweek. Mondays and Tuesdays are my time for writing and filming. Zero appointments are allowed those days, no matter how exciting or important. Thursdays and Fridays after 11:00 a.m. are when I allow a select few meetings. These include coaching calls, podcasts, or calls with relevant people.

Getting your schedule to reflect your Future Self is a major and important step that very few people fully embrace. It will never be convenient to stop the firehose of lesser goals. They will never stop coming. Most externally successful people still fall into the trap of being managed by time, rather than owning and creating their experience of time.

Whenever I increase ownership of my time, I became less willing to waste minutes on lesser goals. Things I'd say "Yes" to a month ago are absolute no-go's today. I whittle more and more from my schedule and tighten the filter on what Chelsea allows on my calendar.

You don't need an assistant to do this.

You don't need to be self-employed.

Time freedom starts with a decision, and is a perpetual refinement.

Are you willing to put the important before the urgent? Are you committed to your current self or your Future Self? Are you driven by short-term and urgent battles, or lifting your gaze to be your Future Self now?

Without question, taking ownership of your time demands commitment and courage. Busy can be a comfort zone despite knowing you're being ineffective. Living busy and trapped in lesser goals allows you to avoid the truth of your Future Self. Steven Pressfield calls this resistance. As he states in *The War of Art*:

> Procrastination is the most common manifestation of Resistance because it's the easiest to rationalize. We don't tell ourselves, "I'm never going to write my symphony." Instead, we say, "I am going to write my symphony; I'm just going to start tomorrow." . . . The more important a call or action to our soul's evolution, the more Resistance we will feel toward pursuing it.[28]

Once you commit to your Future Self, you'll be required to be courageous. Choosing freedom over security is an act of courage.

Are there risks?

Of course.

Every time you choose your Future Self over your current self, there is risk. But being your Future Self now and doing what your Future Self would do immediately creates results beyond anything you've done before.

Yes, with deliberate practice comes failure.

Yes, being in the arena can lead to battle scars.

It's better to fail at the level of your Future Self than succeed as your current self.

How much does your schedule reflect your Future Self?

How much does your schedule reflect your priorities? To repeat Jim Collins, "If you have more than three priorities, you have none."[29]

Once you've clarified your three priorities, it's time to live them.

Schedule time.

Own your time.

AGGRESSIVELY COMPLETE IMPERFECT WORK

"If you're planning to do something with your life, if you have a 10-year plan of how to get there, you should ask: why can't you do this in 6 months?"

—Peter Theil[30]

"Ship often. Ship lousy stuff, but ship. Ship constantly. Skip meetings. Often. Skip them with impunity. Ship."

—Seth Godin[31]

Seth Godin is one of the most prolific and innovative business thinkers of the 21st century. In 1999, he published *Permission Marketing*, a revolutionary and humane concept that focuses on having people give you permission to market to them, rather than aggressively interrupting their lives with your marketing.[32]

In 2003, Godin published *Purple Cow*, a bold invitation to stop being boring with the products you make and how you market them. Why be a brown cow when you could be a purple one? There is risk in being bold and standing out.

He stated:

If you're remarkable, it's likely that some people won't like you. That's part of the definition of remarkable. Nobody gets unanimous praise—ever. The best the timid can hope for is to be unnoticed. Criticism comes to those who stand out.[33]

Godin utilized the idea of *Purple Cow* in his book launch. The first self-published edition came packaged in a milk carton for the cost of shipping and handling. With words printed sideways on a purple and white cover, the title sold over 150,000 copies in 23 printings over the first two years of release.

In 2007, Godin published *The Dip*, an explanation of why being the best in the world is seriously underrated, and how to do it.[34] To be the best, you must know when to stick with something and when to quit.

As he said:

Sometimes we get discouraged and turn to inspirational writing, like stuff from Vince Lombardi:

"Quitters never win and winners never quit." Bad advice. Winners quit all the time. They just quit the right stuff at the right time.

Quit your lesser goals.

Quit anything that isn't taking you closer to the mountain.

Don't stick with something just because your former self invested in it.

Quit everything that isn't living as your Future Self.

Godin published *Tribes* in 2008, a leadership manifesto, and *Linchpin* in 2010, a book about becoming indispensable in your work.[35] In *Linchpin*, Godin introduced his idea of *shipping*, which he borrowed from a Steve Jobs quote, "Real artists ship."

For Godin, here's what it means to ship:

> *The only purpose of starting is to finish*, and while the projects we do are never really finished they must ship. Shipping means hitting the *publish* button on your blog, showing a presentation to the sales team, answering the phone, selling the muffins, sending out your references. Shipping is the collision between your work and the outside world.

Consistently shipping is what enables you to get to your best work. Shipping keeps you going. As Godin continued:

> Shipping isn't focused on producing a master-piece (but all master-pieces get shipped). I've produced more than a hundred books (most didn't sell very well), but if I hadn't, I'd never have had the chance to write this one. Picasso painted more than

a thousand paintings, and you can probably name three of them.

So far in Godin's story, I've only referenced a few of his most popular works. He published more than 20 books and thousands of posts on his daily blog. Godin ships every single day.

Shipping is about finishing. Done is better than perfect. To quote Leonardo da Vinci, "Art is never finished, only abandoned."

To finish, you release your imperfect work. You send your art into the world. You market. And you ship more.

Godin said:

> Sometimes, shipping feels like a compromise. You set out to make a difference, to create art that matters and to do your best work. Then a deadline arrives and you have to cut the work short. Is shipping that important? I think it is. I think the discipline of shipping is essential in the long-term path of becoming indispensable.

Godin's story and ideas bring us to the 7th and final step of being your Future Self, and that is *aggressive completion*.

The completion of projects. The completion of goals and objectives.

Imperfect completion.

Consistent completion.

The completion of better and better projects.

To become your Future Self, you can't stay outside the arena. Move outside paralysis by analysis in your head and enter into the arena where you ship your work.

As beautiful as you are, your current self is incredibly limited and ignorant. The best work you can produce now is pebbles to what your Future Self will create. Your Future Self gives you permission to produce.

Nothing you produce will be perfect. Everything you produce will be from the limited perspective of where you are in a given moment. The books I wrote three years ago aren't the books I'd write today. If you spoke to me a few years after I finished this book, you'd talk to a different Ben Hardy. My Future Self is a different person.

So is yours.

Shipping is how you reach your Future Self. Staying attached to your former work or your former views keeps you stuck.

To quote Adam Grant in *Think Again*:

> To unlock the joy of being wrong, we need to detach. I've learned that two kinds of detachment are especially useful: detaching your present from your past and detaching your opinions from your identity . . . My past self was Mr. Facts—I was too fixated on knowing. Now I'm more interested in finding out what I don't know. As Bridgewater founder, Ray Dalio told me, "If you don't look back at yourself and think, 'Wow, how stupid I was a year ago,' then you must not have learned much in the past year."[36]

I love Grant's and Dalio's sentiments, although I disagree with Dalio's tone. There's no value in demeaning or disrespecting your past, current, or Future Self.

Your former self was more limited in their scope and experience than your current self.

Your current self is dramatically limited relative to your Future Self.

Let this truth liberate you.

There are two fundamental principles for continuous completion. Apply these principles consistently to invest in loss and make exponential progress toward your Future Self.

1. **Parkinson's Law:** Work fills the space you give it. If you give yourself three years to complete something, completion will take three years. If you give yourself three months, there's probably a pathway.

2. **The 80 Percent Rule:** Done is better than perfect. Dan Sullivan explained, "Eighty percent gets results, while 100 percent is still thinking about it."

Perfectionism leads to procrastination. "Eighty percent gets results."

When we put a man on the moon, we didn't have anything near the technology and science we have now. We innovated until we had the tools to get us on the moon. There's no way we'd use the same tools now we used back then.

Prolific is better than perfect.

The more you make completion a way of life, the more you become your Future Self.

Eighty percent to your current self is beyond anything your former self could ever do.

Eighty percent to your Future Self will be beyond anything your current self could do.

Confidence comes from completion.

Completion requires commitment.

Anyone can start, but few finish. The further you go, the less competition there will be. Most people succumbed to their lesser goals and gave up a long time ago.

Every step you take toward your Future Self puts you in rarer air.

Everything you complete teaches you something you'll use for the next project.

Become a master of completing and shipping. If you don't, then your Future Self will be an idea but not a fact.

FUTURE SELF STEPS

Your Future Self compounds in whatever directions you decide and focus.

The simpler and clearer your Future Self, the more focused you'll be now.

In this section of the book, we've just covered the seven steps to being your Future Self now. These steps will enable you to clarify, prioritize, and be your desired Future Self.

These steps are simple and clear, but take continual work and refinement.

As you apply the steps, your life will quickly change. Every day you'll live with more intention and commitment. You'll weed out lesser goals. You'll have a more definite attitude about your Future Self.

You'll increasingly know that what you want is yours.

Your system will change, enabling you to create incredible results with increased ease and flow.

Your schedule will change, reflecting your priorities instead of lesser goals.

You'll become increasingly productive and prolific, creating ever better work.

BE YOUR FUTURE SELF NOW

"Freedom lies in being bold."

—Robert Frost[1]

On September 1, 2012, Lauren and I got married. Exactly one year later, we made a 9-year time capsule of where we imagined we'd be 10 years from our wedding day.

We wrote letters to our Future Selves and filmed videos saying where we thought our lives would be. We placed our letters and video files into a mason jar and it has waited on the shelf in our living room ever since.

As I write these words, today is January 13, 2022. Later this year, we will open our nine-year time capsule and see what we recorded. I'm motivated to make as much progress as I can before we open the jar, knowing the pending date is fast approaching. I'm eager to see how close our predictions were, and how different our lives are from what we thought they would be.

Nine years ago, Lauren and I had just finished our undergrad degrees. We lived in the basement of her parents' home. No less than 15 Ph.D. programs had rejected my application. The future felt uncertain. I knew I wanted to be an author, but wouldn't start that process for nearly three more years.

We did not have children. I wasn't an entrepreneur, nor did I plan on becoming one. Little did we know we would adopt three siblings from the foster system and have three more of our own. Little did we know my writing career would take off as it did.

I have no clue what we said in our time capsule, but I'm certain the life we created is far beyond anything our former selves imagined.

At the beginning of this book, I shared the story of Jimmy (MrBeast) Donaldson and the four time-capsule videos he filmed to his Future Self. He filmed a 6-month Future

Self time capsule, a 12-month time capsule, 5-year time capsule, and 10-year time capsule.

In 2020, his five-year "Hi Me in Five Years" published on his YouTube channel. The younger Jimmy dreamed he'd have one million YouTube subscribers when his five-year time capsule aired. Instead, he had more than 44 million subscribers. He wildly out performed his greatest ideals.

As we come to the end of our time together, I have one final invitation for you. In the next 24 hours, give yourself some space and make a time capsule of some form for your Future Self. Like Jimmy, you can film a video and set the recording to publish on a future date. You can write yourself a letter and store the message in a jar on the shelf like Lauren and I did.

The mode matters far less than that you do it.

For example, on January 1 of every year, my friend Lee Brower films a short video speaking as his Future Self one year in the future. The future Lee starts by saying, "Lee, if you're seeing this, then you've made it another year." Future Lee then lists everything that happened during that year. One year later, Lee watches the video to see how close he lived to what he said would happen. Then, he films his video for the coming year.

You can create multiple time capsules. A 6-month time capsule, 12 month, 3 year, 5 year, 10 year, 20 year. Your time capsule is your final *Be Your Future Self Now* call to action. Compile a time capsule today for the time frame you choose. Make your vision clear and bold. Utilize the principles you learned in this book to connect to and clarify your Future Self. Define your core three priorities.

Know that despite your best predictions, your Future Self will likely be far different than you anticipate. Life will teach you more than you expect. Your Future Self is wiser than your present self can imagine.

With your time capsule in place, be your Future Self now.

Being is the first step of doing.

Do what your Future Self will do.

Know that what you want is already yours.

Commit 100 percent to your desired Future Self.

Remove lesser goals.

Turn every experience along the way into a gain.

Cheers to your Future Self.

Congratulations on the investment you made by reading this book.

Go now, and be your Future Self.

(ENDNOTES)

Introduction

1. Goddard, N. (2015). *The Power of Unlimited Imagination: A Collection of Neville's San Francisco Lectures.* Devorss & Co.

2. MrBeast. (2016). *Dear Future Me (Scheduled Uploaded 6 Months Ago).* MrBeast YouTube Channel. Accessed on August 13, 2021 at https://www.youtube.com/watch?v=fG1N5kzcAhM

3. MrBeast. (2016). *BEST INTROS ON YOUTUBE #1.* MrBeast YouTube Channel. Accessed on August 13, 2021 at https://www.youtube.com/watch?v=tqO3_AKC5Ks

4. MrBeast. (2016). *CUTTING TABLE IN HALF WITH PLASTIC KNIVES.* MrBeast YouTube Channel. Accessed on August 13, 2021 at https://www.youtube.com/watch?v=tqO3_AKC5Ks

5. MrBeast. (2016). *100 LAYERS OF SARAN WRAP + TOILET PAPER!!.* MrBeast YouTube Channel. Accessed on August 13, 2021 at https://www.youtube.com/watch?v=bqpKlkPpT10

6. MrBeast. (2016). *IF ONLINE ADS WERE REAL.* MrBeast YouTube Channel. Accessed on August 13, 2021 at https://www.youtube.com/watch?v=NEDPgQYhbqs

7. MrBeast. (2017). *I Counted To 100,000!* MrBeast YouTube Channel. Accessed on August 13, 2021 at https://www.youtube.com/watch?v=xWcldHxHFpo

8. MrBeast. (2017). *Counting To 200,000 (Road To A Mil).* MrBeast YouTube Channel. Accessed on August 13, 2021 at https://www.youtube.com/watch?v=9CVwXBYVqVk

9. MrBeast. (2017). *Counting To 300,000 Road To A Mil (Part 1).* MrBeast YouTube Channel. Accessed on August 13, 2021 at https://www.youtube.com/watch?v=0SNiEDWRnEQ

10. MrBeast. (2017). *Saying Logan Paul 100,000 Times.* MrBeast YouTube Channel. Accessed on August 13, 2021 at https://www.youtube.com/watch?v=_FX6rml2Yjs

11. MrBeast. (2017). *Giving A Random Homeless Man $10,000.* MrBeast YouTube Channel. Accessed on August 13, 2021 at https://www.youtube.com/watch?v=N_GMakKf7G4

12. MrBeast. (2017). *Giving Homeless People $1,000 (Not Clickbait).* MrBeast YouTube Channel. Accessed on August 13, 2021 at https://www.youtube.com/watch?v=4KVmSG6KS2k

13. MrBeast. (2017). *Donating $10,000 To Random Twitch Streamers.* MrBeast YouTube Channel. Accessed on August 13, 2021 at https://www.youtube.com/watch?v=kupaqq-xJ_8

14. MrBeast. (2017). *Tipping Pizza Delivery Guys $10,000.* MrBeast YouTube Channel. Accessed on August 13, 2021 at https://www.youtube.com/watch?v=uotb9ZHnI2g

15. MrBeast. (2017). *Tipping Uber Drivers $10,000.* MrBeast YouTube Channel. Accessed on August 13, 2021 at https://www.youtube.com/watch?v=zAAXW7ySu1k

16. MrBeast. (2017). *How Many Balloons Does It Take To Float?* MrBeast YouTube Channel. Accessed on August 13, 2021 at https://www.youtube.com/watch?v=8bYzXI7bb8k8bYzXI7bb8k

17. MrBeast. (2018). *I Bought One Snickers Bar From Every Walmart.* MrBeast YouTube Channel. Accessed on August 13, 2021 at https://www.youtube.com/watch?v=sirrTXiPFmw

18. MrBeast. (2018). *I Bought One Snickers Bar From Every Walmart.* MrBeast YouTube Channel. Accessed on August 13, 2021 at https://www.youtube.com/watch?v=nLpqZEAFnkE

19. MrBeast. (2018). *Giving 3,000,000 Pennies To My 3,000,000th Subscriber.* MrBeast YouTube Channel. Accessed on August 13, 2021 at https://www.youtube.com/watch?v=Pe3pGsCeYXg

20. Seligman, M. E., Railton, P., Baumeister, R. F., & Sripada, C. (2013). Navigating into the future or driven by the past. *Perspectives on Psychological Science*, 8(2), 119–141.

21. Baer, J., Kaufman, J. C., & Baumeister, R. F. (Eds.). (2008). *Are We Free? Psychology and Free Will.* Oxford University Press.

22. Slife, B. D., & Fisher, A. M. (2000). Modern and postmodern approaches to the free will/determinism dilemma in psychotherapy. *Journal of Humanistic Psychology*, 40(1), 80–107.

23. Slife, B. (2002). Time, information, and determinism in psychology. *Between Chance and Choice: Interdisciplinary Perspectives on Determinism*, 469–83.

24. Richardson, F., & Bishop, R. (2002). Rethinking determinism in social science. *Between Chance and Choice: Interdisciplinary Perspectives on Determinism*, 425–45.

25. Seligman, M. E., Railton, P., Baumeister, R. F., & Sripada, C. (2013). Navigating into the future or driven by the past. *Perspectives on Psychological Science*, 8(2), 119–141.

26. Seligman, M. E., Railton, P., Baumeister, R. F., & Sripada, C. (2016). *Homo prospectus.* Oxford University Press.

27. Gilbert, D. T., & Wilson, T. D. (2007). Prospection: Experiencing the future. *Science*, 317(5843), 1351–1354.

28. Rosenblueth, A., Wiener, N., & Bigelow, J. (1943). Behavior, purpose and teleology. *Philosophy of Science*, 10(1), 18–24.

29. Coats, E. J., Janoff-Bulman, R., & Alpert, N. (1996). Approach versus avoidance goals: Differences in self-evaluation and well-being. *Personality and Social Psychology Bulletin*, 22(10), 1057–1067.

30. Elliot, A. J., & Friedman, R. (2017). Approach—Avoidance: A Central Characteristic 01 Personal Goals. *In Personal Project Pursuit Goals, Action, and Human Flourishing* (pp. 97–118). Psychology Press.

31. Hawkins, D. R. (2015). *Healing and Recovery*. Hay House.

32. 50 Cent & Greene, R. (2009). *The 50th Law*. Amistad.

33. The Weekend University. (2021). *The Psychology of Your Future Self—Professor Hal Hershfield*. Accessed on October 4, 2021, at https://www.youtube.com/watch?v=QBdIeC7FYkU

34. Statistica. (2019). *Life expectancy (from birth) in the United States, from 1860 to 2020**. Accessed on October 4, 2021, https://www.statista.com/statistics/1040079/life-expectancy-united-states-all-time/

35. Gilbert, D. (2014). *The psychology of your Future Self*. TED Talk. Retrieved on December 7, 2021, at https://www.ted.com/talks/dan_gilbert_the_psychology_of_your_future_self?language=en

36. Goldstien, D. (2011). *The battle between your present and Future Self*. TED Talk. Retrieved on December 7, 2021, at https://www.ted.com/talks/daniel_goldstein_the_battle_between_your_present_and_future_self

37. Jay, M. (2021). *Essential questions to ask your Future Self*. TED Talk. Retrieved on December 7, 2021, at https://www.ted.com/talks/meg_jay_essential_questions_to_ask_your_future_self?language=en

38. Da Sliva, A. (2020). *A journey to your Future Self*. TED Talk. Retrieved on December 7, 2021, at https://www.ted.com/talks/alex_da_sliva_a_journey_to_your_future_self

39. Stewart, J. M. (2020). *Guidance from your Future Self*. TED Talk. Retrieved on December 7, 2021, at https://www.ted.com/talks/mark_john_stewart_guidance_from_your_future_self

40. Howard, J. (2019). *Saying hello to your Future Self*. TED Talk. Retrieved on December 7, 2021, at https://www.ted.com/talks/jon_howard_saying_hello_to_your_future_self

41. Hershfield, H. (2014). How can we help our future selves? TEDxEast. Retrieved on December 7, 2021, at https://www.youtube.com/watch?v=tJotBbd7MwQ&t

42. Wilson, D. (2016). *Thinking Forward For Your Future Self: Establishing Your i+1* | Diamond Wilson | TEDxPlano. Retrieved on December 7, 2021, at https://www.youtube.com/watch?v=2_zMc9T4ekA

43. Maciejovsky, B. (2015). *How to make our Present self become our Future Self* | Boris Maciejovsky | TEDxUCR. Retreived on December 7, 2021, at https://www.youtube.com/watch?v=avTD-NyCSUI

44. Mudathir, M. (2020). *Challenge your Future Self* | MATHANI MUDATHIR | TEDxYouth@TWSDubai. Retrieved on December 7, 2021, at https://www.youtube.com/watch?v=rTmj34G3K0M

45. Plewa, P. (2020). *How To Step Into Your Future Self* | Pauly Plewa | TEDxMcMasterU. Retrieved on December 7, 2021, at https://www.youtube.com/watch?v=w8AzABQ_2_0

46. Hershfield, H. E., Goldstein, D. G., Sharpe, W. F., Fox, J., Yeykelis, L., Carstensen, L. L., & Bailenson, J. N. (2011). Increasing saving behavior through age-progressed renderings of the Future Self. *Journal of Marketing Research*, 48(SPL), S23-S37.

47. Rutchick, A. M., Slepian, M. L., Reyes, M. O., Pleskus, L. N., & Hershfield, H. E. (2018). Future Self-continuity is associated with improved health and increases exercise behavior. *Journal of Experimental Psychology: Applied*, 24(1), 72.

48. Van Gelder, J. L., Hershfield, H. E., & Nordgren, L. F. (2013). Vividness of the Future Self predicts delinquency. *Psychological Science*, 24(6), 974-980.

49. Van Berkum, J. J. (2010). The brain is a prediction machine that cares about good and bad-any implications for neuropragmatics? *Italian Journal of Linguistics*, 22, 181-208.

50. Den Ouden, H. E., Kok, P., & De Lange, F. P. (2012). How prediction errors shape perception, attention, and motivation. *Frontiers in Psychology*, 3, 548.

51. Long, T. L. (Writer), & Kruse, N. (Director). (2010). "Money Bart" [Television series episode]. In A. Jean, J. Frink, J. L. Brooks, M. Groening, M. Selman, & S. Simon (Producers), *The Simpsons*.

52. Letterman, D. (1994). *Jerry Seinfeld—Night Guy/Morning Guy*. Accessed on October 4, 2021 at https://jerryseinfeldarchives.tumblr.com/post/155428911272/night-guymorning-guy-letterman-1994

53. Hershfield, H. E., Cohen, T. R., & Thompson, L. (2012). Short horizons and tempting situations: Lack of continuity to our future selves leads to unethical decision making and behavior. *Organizational Behavior and Human Decision Processes*, 117 (2), 298–310.

54. Gilbert, D. (2013). *The Psychology of Your Future Self*. Filmed 2014 in Vancouver, BC. TED video, 6:49. Accessed on October 4, 2021, https://www.ted.com/talks/dan_gilbert_the_psychology_of_your_future_self

55. Frankl, V. E. (1985). *Man's Search for Meaning*. Simon & Schuster.

56. Anders Ericsson, K. (2008). Deliberate practice and acquisition of expert performance: a general overview. *Academic Emergency Medicine*, 15(11), 988-994.

57. Ericsson, A., & Pool, R. (2016). *Peak: Secrets from the New Science of Expertise.* Houghton Mifflin Harcourt.

58. Suddendorf, T., Brinums, M., & Imuta, K. (2016). *Shaping One's Future Self: The Development of Deliberate Practice.*

59. Covey, S. R. (2013). *The 7 Habits of Highly Effective People: Powerful Lessons in Personal Change.* Simon & Schuster.

60. Hebrews 11:1. King James Bible.

61. Johnston, W. A., & Dark, V. J. (1986). Selective attention. *Annual Review of Psychology, 37*(1), 43-75.

62. James, W. (1863). *Principles of Psychology.* Dover Publications, Inc.

63. Shinn, F. S. (2009). *The Game of Life and How to Play It.* Penguin.

64. Dethmer, J., Chapman, D., & Klemp, K. (2014). *The 15 Commitments of Conscious Leadership: A New Paradigm for Sustainable Success.* Conscious Leadership Group.

Part 1

1. Godin, S. (2012). *The Icarus Deception: How High Will You Fly?* Penguin.

2. Frankl, V. E. (1985). *Man's Search for Meaning.* Simon & Schuster.

3. Frankl, V. E. (1985). *Man's Search for Meaning.* Simon & Schuster.

4. Arden, P. (2003). *It's Not How Good You Are, It's How Good You Want to Be.* Phaidon Press.

5. Frankl, V. E. (1985). *Man's Search for Meaning.* Simon & Schuster.

6. Baumeister, R. F., & Vohs, K. D. (2002). The pursuit of meaningfulness in life. *Handbook of Positive Psychology, 1,* 608–618.

7. Proverbs 29:18. King James Bible.

8. Duckworth, A. (2016). *Grit: The Power of Passion and Perseverance.* New York, NY: Scribner.

9. Reichard, R. J., Avey, J. B., Lopez, S., & Dollwet, M. (2013). Having the will and finding the way: A review and meta-analysis of hope at work. *The Journal of Positive Psychology, 8*(4), 292–304.

10. Tong, E. M., Fredrickson, B. L., Chang, W., & Lim, Z. X. (2010). Re-examining hope: The roles of agency thinking and pathways thinking. *Cognition and Emotion, 24* (7), 1207–1215.

11. Bryant, F. B., & Cvengros, J. A. (2004). Distinguishing hope and optimism: Two sides of a coin, or two separate coins? *Journal of Social and Clinical Psychology, 23* (2), 273–302.

12. Fischer, I. C., Cripe, L. D., & Rand, K. L. (2018). Predicting symptoms of anxiety and depression in patients living with advanced cancer: The differential roles of hope and optimism. *Supportive Care in Cancer, 26*(10), 3471–3477.

13. Fowler, D. R., Weber, E. N., Klappa, S. P., & Miller, S. A. (2017). Replicating future orientation: Investigating the constructs of hope and optimism and their subscales through replication and expansion. *Personality and Individual Differences*, 116, 22–28.

14. Chang, E. C. (1998). Hope, problem-solving ability, and coping in a college student population: Some implications for theory and practice. *Journal of Clinical Psychology*, 54(7), 953–962.

15. Snyder, C. R., LaPointe, A. B., Jeffrey Crowson, J., & Early, S. (1998). Preferences of high- and low-hope people for self-referential input. *Cognition & Emotion*, 12(6), 807–823.

16. Snyder, C. R., Shorey, H. S., Cheavens, J., Pulvers, K. M., Adams III, V. H., & Wiklund, C. (2002). Hope and academic success in college. *Journal of Educational Psychology*, 94(4), 820.

17. Levine, P. A. (1997). *Waking the Tiger: Healing Trauma: The Innate Capacity to Transform Overwhelming Experiences.* North Atlantic Books.

18. Livingston, G. (2009). *Too Soon Old, Too Late Smart: Thirty True Things You Need to Know Now.* Da Capo Lifelong Books.

19. Faulkner, W. (2011). *Requiem for a Nun.* Vintage.

20. Slife, B. D. (1993). *Time and Psychological Explanation: The Spectacle of Spain's Tourist Boom and the Reinvention of Difference.* SUNY Press.

21. Tedeschi, R. G., Shakespeare-Finch, J., Taku, K., & Calhoun, L. G. (2018). *Posttraumatic Growth: Theory, Research, and Applications.* Routledge.

22. Sullivan, D. & Hardy, B. (2021). *The Gap and the Gain: The High Achievers' Guide to Confidence, Happiness, and Success.* Hay House Business.

23. Rosenthal, R., & Jacobson, L. (1968). Pygmalion in the classroom. *The Urban Review*, 3(1), 16–20.

24. Boyd, R., & MacNeill, N. (2020). How Teachers' Self-Fulfilling Prophecies, Known as the Pygmalion Effect, Influence Students' Success. *Education Today*, 24.

25. Szumski, G., & Karwowski, M. (2019). Exploring the Pygmalion effect: The role of teacher expectations, academic self-concept, and class context in students' math achievement. *Contemporary Educational Psychology*, 59, 101787.

26. Berger, J. (2016). *Invisible Influence: The Hidden Forces That Shape Behavior.* Simon & Schuster.

27. Bornstein, R. F., & D'agostino, P. R. (1992). Stimulus recognition and the mere exposure effect. *Journal of Personality and Social Psychology*, 63(4), 545.

28. Fang, X., Singh, S., & Ahluwalia, R. (2007). An examination of different explanations for the mere exposure effect. *Journal of Consumer Research*, 34(1), 97–103.

29. Bornstein, R. F., & Craver-Lemley, C. (2016). Mere exposure effect. In *Cognitive Illusions* (pp. 266–285). Psychology Press.

30. Morgenstern, M., Isensee, B., & Hanewinkel, R. (2013). Seeing and liking cigarette advertisements: is there a 'mere exposure'effect? *European Addiction Research*, 19(1), 42–46.

31. Langer, E. J. (2014). *Mindfulness*. Da Capo Lifelong Books.

32. Goldsmith, M., & Reiter, M. (2015). *Triggers: Creating Behavior That Lasts--Becoming the Person You Want to Be* (Vol. 37, No. 7). Currency.

33. Frankl, V. E. (1985). *Man's Search for Meaning*. Simon & Schuster.

34. Langer, E. J. (2009). *Counterclockwise: Mindful Health and the Power of Possibility*. Ballantine Books.

35. Johnston, W. A., & Dark, V. J. (1986). Selective attention. *Annual Review of Psychology*, 37(1), 43–75.

36. Mack, A. (2003). Inattentional blindness: Looking without seeing. *Current Directions in Psychological Science*, 12(5), 180–184.

37. Duckworth, A. (2016). *Grit: The Power of Passion and Perseverance. Part III: Growing Grit from the Outside In*. New York, NY: Scribner.

38. The Weekend University. (2021). *The Psychology of Your Future Self— Professor Hal Hershfield*. Accessed on October 4, 2021, at https://www.youtube.com/watch?v=QBdIeC7FYkU

39. Blouin-Hudon, E. M. C., & Pychyl, T. A. (2017). A mental imagery intervention to increase Future Self-continuity and reduce procrastination. *Applied Psychology*, 66(2), 326–352.

40. Van Gelder, J. L., Luciano, E. C., Weulen Kranenbarg, M., & Hershfield, H. E. (2015). Friends with my Future Self: Longitudinal vividness intervention reduces delinquency. *Criminology*, 53(2), 158–179.

41. 50 Cent & Greene, R. (2009). *The 50th Law*. Amistad.

42. Cardone, G. (2011). *The 10X Rule: The Only Difference Between Success and Failure*. John Wiley & Sons.

43. Simons, D. J., & Chabris, C. F. (1999). Gorillas in our midst: Sustained inattentional blindness for dynamic events. *Perception*, 28(9), 1059–1074.

44. Mack, A. (2003). Inattentional blindness: Looking without seeing. *Current Directions in Psychological Science*, 12(5), 180–184.

45. Dyer, W. W. (2010). *The Power of Intention: Learning to Co-Create Your World Your Way*. Hay House, Inc.

46. Arden, P. (2003). *It's Not How Good You Are, It's How Good You Want to Be*. Phaidon Press.

47. Hardy, D. (2011). *The Compound Effect*. Vanguard Press.

48. Rate, C. R., Clarke, J. A., Lindsay, D. R., & Sternberg, R. J. (2007). Implicit theories of courage. *The Journal of Positive Psychology*, 2(2), 80–98.

49. Rate, C. R. (2010). Defining the features of courage: A search for meaning. *The Psychology Of Courage: Modern Research on an Ancient Virtue*, 47, 66.

50. Hawkins, D. R. (2014). Power Vs. Force: The Hidden Determinants of Human Behavior. Hay House, Inc.

51. Walsh, B., Jamison, S., & Walsh, C. (2009). *The Score Takes Care of Itself: My Philosophy of Leadership*. Penguin.

52. Hendricks, G., & Hendricks, G. (2009). *The Big Leap*. HarperCollins.

53. McKeown, G. (2014). *Essentialism: The Disciplined Pursuit of Less*. Currency.

54. Brault, R. (2014). *Round Up The Usual Subjects: Thoughts On Just About Everything*.

55. Hopf, G. M. (2016). *Those Who Remain: A Postapocalyptic Novel (The New World Series Book 7)*. CreateSpace Independent Publishing Platform.

56. Durant, W., & Durant, A. (2012). *The Lessons of History*. Simon & Schuster.

57. Dalio, R. (2021). *Principles for Dealing with the Changing World Order: Why Nations Succeed and Fail*. Simon & Schuster.

58. James 1:8. King James Bible.

Part 2

1. Frankl, V. E. (1985). *Man's Search for Meaning*. Simon & Schuster.

2. "Greatest robbery of a Government". Guinness World Records. Retrieved December 21, 2021 at https://www.guinnessworldrecords .com/world-records/65607-greatest-robbery-of-a-government

3. Durant, W., & Durant, A. (2012). *The Lessons of History*. Simon & Schuster.

4. Charlton, W., & Hussey, E. (1999). *Aristotle Physics Book VIII (Vol. 3)*. Oxford University Press.

5. Turnbull, R. G. (1958). Aristotle's Debt to the 'Natural Philosophy' of the Phaedo. *Philosophical Quarterly*, 8, 131–143.

6. Scharle, M. (2008). Elemental Teleology in Aristotle's Physics II 8. *Oxford Studies in Ancient Philosophy*, 34, 147–184.

7. Boeri, M. D. (1995). Change and Teleology in Aristotle Physics. *International Philosophical Quarterly*, 34, 87–96.

8. Charles, D. (1991). Teleological Causation in the Physics, in L. Judson (ed.), *Aristotle's Physics: A Collection of Essays*. Oxford: Oxford University Press, 101–128.

9. Charles, D. (2012). Teleological Causation, in C. Shields (ed.), *The Oxford Handbook of Aristotle*. Oxford: Oxford University Press, 227–266.

10. Rosenblueth, A., Wiener, N., & Bigelow, J. (1943). Behavior, purpose and teleology. *Philosophy of Science*, 10(1), 18–24.

11. Thiel, P. A., & Masters, B. (2014). *Zero to One: Notes on Startups, or How to Build the Future*. Currency.

12. Clear, J. (2018). *Atomic Habits: Tiny Changes, Remarkable Results: An Easy & Proven Way to Build Good Habits & Break Bad Ones*. Avery.

13. Howes, L. (2018). *James Clear: Success Habits: The Proven Way to Achieve Your Dreams*. Retrieved on December 30, 2021 at https://lewishowes.com/podcast/the-proven-way-to-achieve-your-dreams-with-james-clear/

14. Clear, J. (2019). *3-2-1: On systems vs. goals, endings, and the importance of leverage*. Retrieved on January 11, 2022, at https://jamesclear.com/3-2-1/december-31-2020

15. Perttula, A., Kiili, K., Lindstedt, A., & Tuomi, P. (2017). Flow experience in game based learning—a systematic literature review. *International Journal of Serious Games, 4*(1).

16. Csikszentmihalyi, M., Abuhamdeh, S., & Nakamura, J. (2014). *Flow and the Foundations of Positive Psychology*. 227–238. Springer, Dordrecht.

17. Kotler, S. (2014). *The Rise of Superman: Decoding the Science of Ultimate Human Performance*. Houghton Mifflin Harcourt.

18. Frankl, V. E. (1985). *Man's Search for Meaning*. Simon & Schuster.

19. Gilbert, D. (2014). *The Psychology of your Future Self*. TED Talk.

20. Gilbert, D. (2006). *Stumbling Upon Happiness*. Knopf.

21. Gilbert, D. (2014). *The Psychology of your Future Self*. TED Talk.

22. Gilbert, D. (2014). *The Psychology of your Future Self*. TED Talk.

23. Quoidbach, J., Gilbert, D. T., & Wilson, T. D. (2013). The end of history illusion. *Science, 339*(6115), 96–98.

24. Harris, H., & Busseri, M. A. (2019). Is there an 'end of history illusion' for life satisfaction? Evidence from a three-wave longitudinal study. *Journal of Research in Personality*, 83, 103869.

25. Dweck, C. S. (2008). *Mindset: The New Psychology of Success*. Random House Digital, Inc.

26. Einstein, A. (2010). *The Ultimate Quotable Einstein*. Princeton University Press.

27. Olson, J. (2013). *The Slight Edge*. Greenleaf Book Group.

28. Sitzmann, T., & Yeo, G. (2013). A meta-analytic investigation of the within-person self-efficacy domain: Is self-efficacy a product of past performance or a driver of future performance? *Personnel Psychology*, 66(3), 531–568.

29. Fogg, BJ (2020). *Tiny Habits: The Small Shanges That Change Everything.* Houghton Mifflin Harcourt.

30. Berk, L. E. (2010). *Exploring Lifespan Development (2nd ed.).* 314. Pearson Education Inc.

31. Hardy, B. (2016). *Does It Take Courage to Start a Business?*

32. Bodner, R., & Prelec, D. (2003). Self-signaling and diagnostic utility in everyday decision making. *The Psychology of Economic Decisions,* 1(105), 26.

33. Hawkins, D. R. (2014). *Letting Go: The Pathway of Surrender.* Hay House, Inc.

34. Baer, D. (2013). *How Arianna Huffington networks without networking.* Fast Company. Retrieved on June 3, 2021, at https:// www.fastcompany .com/3018307/how-arianna-huffington-networks-without-networking

35. Ferriss, T. (2017). *Tools of Titans: The Tactics, Routines, and Habits of Billionaires, Icons, and World-Class Performers.* Houghton Mifflin.

36. Souman, J. L., Frissen, I., Sreenivasa, M. N., & Ernst, M. O. (2009). Walking straight into circles. *Current Biology,* 19(18), 1538–1542.

37. Max Plank Institute. (2009). *Walking in circles Scientists from Tübingen show that people really walk in circles when lost.* Max Planck Institute for Biological Cybernetics. Accessed on October 6, 2021 at https://www .mpg.de/596269/pressRelease200908171

38. Max Plank Institute. (2009). *Walking in circles: Scientists from Tübingen show that people really walk in circles when lost.* Max Planck Institute for Biological Cybernetics. Accessed on October 6, 2021 at https://www .mpg.de/596269/pressRelease200908171

39. Horigome, Y. (2019). *Yuto Horigome | Rising Legend of Japanese Skateboarder.* Retrieved on January 10, 2022 at https://www.youtube.com/ watch?v=FaGJbRHuiX0&t

40. Horigome, Y. (2021). *Horigome Yuto: His story and the road to the Tokyo 2020 Olympics.* Retreived on January 10, 2022, at https:// olympics.com/en/news/horigome-yuto-his-story-and-the-road-to-the -tokyo-2020-olympics

41. Waitzkin, J. (2008). *The Art of Learning: An Inner Journey to Optimal Performance.* Simon & Schuster.

42. Waitzkin, J. (2008). *The Art of Learning: An Inner Journey to Optimal Performance.* Simon & Schuster.

43. Moors, A., & De Houwer, J. (2006). Automaticity: a theoretical and conceptual analysis. *Psychological Bulletin,* 132(2), 297.

44. Klöckner, C. A., & Verplanken, B. (2018). Yesterday's habits preventing change for tomorrow? About the influence of automaticity on environmental behavior. *Environmental Psychology: An Introduction,* 238–250.

45. Ericsson, A., & Pool, R. (2016). *Peak: Secrets from the New Science of Expertise.* Random House.

46. Anders Ericsson, K. (2008). Deliberate practice and acquisition of expert performance: a general overview. *Academic Emergency Medicine*, 15(11), 988–994.

47. Suddendorf, T., Brinums, M., & Imuta, K. (2016). *Shaping One's Future Self: The Development of Deliberate Practice.*

48. Waitzkin, J. (2008). *The Art of Learning: An Inner Journey to Optimal Performance.* Simon & Schuster.

49. Ferriss, T. (2020). *Josh Waitzkin on Beginner's Mind, Self-Actualization, and Advice from Your Future Self (#412).* Retrieved on January 11, 2022, at https://tim.blog/2020/02/27/josh-waitzkin-beginners-mind-self-actualization-advice-from-your-future-self/

50. Ferriss, T. (2021). *Josh Waitzkin and Tim Ferriss on The Cave Process, Advice from Future Selves, and Training for an Uncertain Future (#498).* Retrieved on January 11, 2022, at https://tim.blog/2021/02/16/josh-waitzkin 2/

51. Ferriss, T. (2020). *The Tim Ferriss Show Transcripts: Josh Waitzkin on Beginner's Mind, Self-Actualization, and Advice from Your Future Self (#412).* Retrieved on January 10, 2022, at https://tim.blog/2020/03/14/josh-waitzkin-transcript-412/

52. Sivers, D. (2021). *How to Live: 27 conflicting answers and one weird conclusion.* (p. 52). Hit media. Retrieved on January 10, 2022, at https://sive.rs/h

53. Shakespeare, W. (1991). *Hamlet:*[1604]. Oxford Text Archive Core Collection.

54. Hitler, A. (2021). *Mein Kampf.* Diamond Pocket Books Pvt Ltd.

55. Pressfield, S. (2002). *The War of Art: Break Through The Blocks and Win your Inner Creative Battles.* Black Irish Entertainment LLC.

56. Ferriss, T. (2015). *Derek Sivers Reloaded – On Success Habits and Billionaires with Perfect Abs (#128).* Retrieved on January 10, 2022, at https://tim.blog/2015/12/28/derek-sivers-reloaded-on-success-habits-and-billionaires-with-perfect-abs/

57. Galvin, B. M., Randel, A. E., Collins, B. J., & Johnson, R. E. (2018). Changing the focus of locus (of control): A targeted review of the locus of control literature and agenda for future research. *Journal of Organizational Behavior*, 39(7), 820–833.

58. Jacobs-Lawson, J. M., Waddell, E. L., & Webb, A. K. (2011). Predictors of health locus of control in older adults. *Current Psychology*, 30(2), 173–183.

59. Benassi, V. A., Sweeney, P. D., & Dufour, C. L. (1988). Is there a relation between locus of control orientation and depression?. *Journal Of Abnormal Psychology, 97*(3), 357.

60. Pinnock, C. H., Rice, R., Sanders, J., Hasker, W., & Basinger, D. (2010). *The Openness of God: A Biblical Challenge to the Traditional Understanding of God*. InterVarsity Press.

61. Acts 17:29. King James Bible.

62. Romans 8:16–17. King James Bible.

63. Wall, M. (2018). *We're Probably Living in a Simulation, Elon Musk Says*. Space.com. Retrieved on October 6, 2021 at https://www.space.com/41749-elon-musk-living-in-simulation-rogan-podcast.html

64. Carter-Scott, C. (1998). *If Life Is a Game, These Are the Rules*. Harmony.

65. Genesis 1:27. King James Bible.

66. Snow, E. (1845). Eliza R. Snow, "My Father in Heaven," October 1845. Retrieved on January 11, 2022, at https://www.churchhistorianspress.org/the-first-fifty-years-of-relief-society/part-1/1-14

67. Olson, R. E. (2007). Deification in contemporary theology. *Theology Today, 64*(2), 186–200.

68. Hallonsten, G. (2007). Theosis in Recent Research: A Renewal of Interest and a Need for Clarity. *Partakers of the Divine Nature. The History and Development of Deification in the Christian Traditions.*

69. Kharlamov, V. (Ed.). (2011). *Theosis: Deification in Christian Theology, Volume Two (Vol. 156)*. Wipf and Stock Publishers.

70. Irenaeus, Adversus Haereses (Irenaeus Against Heresies), book 4, chapter 38, in The Apostolic Fathers, Justin Martyr, Irenaeus, vol. 1 of *Ante-Nicene Fathers: The Writings of the Fathers Down to A.D. 325*, ed. Alexander Roberts and James Donaldson (Peabody, Massachusetts: Hendrickson Publishers, 1994), 522.

71. Irenaeus, Adversus Haereses (Irenaeus Against Heresies), book 5, chapter 36, in vol. 1, *The Apostolic Fathers*, 567.

72. Lewis. C. S. (1960). "Counting the Cost," *Mere Christianity*. New York: Macmillan, 174–75.

73. Smith, E., * Jones, A. (1805). Know Then That Every Soul Is Free. Retrieved on January 12, 2022, at https://www.churchofjesuschrist.org/music/library/hymns/know-this-that-every-soul-is-free

Part 3

1. Segall, K. (2013). *Insanely Simple: The Obsession That Drives Apple's Ssuccess*. Penguin.

2. Isaacson, W. (2011). *Steve Jobs*. Simon & Schuster.

3. McKeown, G. (2014). *Essentialism: The Disciplined Pursuit of Less*. Currency.

4. Luce, C. B. (1931). Stuffed Shirts by Clare Boothe Brokaw. Chapter 17: *Snobs, New Style*, Quote Page 239, Horace Liveright, New York.

5. Frankl, V. E. (1985). *Man's Search for Meaning*. Simon & Schuster.

6. Collins, J. (2001). *Good to Great: Why Some Companies Make The Leap and Others Don't*. HarperBusiness.

7. Dethmer, J., Chapman, D., & Klemp, K. (2014). *The 15 Commitments of Conscious Leadership: A New Paradigm for Sustainable Success*. Conscious Leadership Group.

8. Lawler III, E. E., & Suttle, J. L. (1973). Expectancy theory and job behavior. *Organizational Behavior and Human Performance*, 9(3), 482–503.

9. Hawkins, D. R. (2014). *Power vs. Force: The Hidden Determinants of Human Behavior*. Hay House, Inc.

10. Shinn, F. S. (2009). *The Game of Life and How to Play It*. Penguin.

11. Hill, N. (2020). *Think and Grow Rich: The Original Classic*. Third Millennium Press.

12. Allen, J. (2008). *As a Man Thinketh*. Create Space Independent Publishing Platform.

13. Berk, L. E. (2010). *Exploring Lifespan Development* (2nd ed.). Pg. 314. Pearson Education Inc.

14. Covey, S. R. (2013). *The 7 Habits of Highly Effective People: Powerful Lessons in Personal Change*. Simon & Schuster.

15. Shenk, J. W. (2014). *Powers of Two: Finding the Essence of innovation in Creative Pairs*. Houghton Mifflin Harcourt.

16. WJS, p. 15.

17. Recollection of John Lyman Smith in JI (March 15, 1892): 172.

18. Madsen, T. (1978). Joseph Smith Lecture 2: Joseph's Personality and Character. BYU Speeches. Retrieved on January 5, 2022, at https://speeches.byu.edu/talks/truman-g-madsen/joseph-smiths-personality-and-character/

19. Meisel, A. (2014). *Less Doing, More Living: Make Everything in Life Easier*. TarcherPerigee.

20. Schwartz, B. (2004, January). *The Paradox Of Choice: Why More is Less*. New York: Ecco.

21. McKeown, G. (2014). *Essentialism: The Disciplined Pursuit of Less*. Currency.

22. Hendricks, G., & Hendricks, G. (2009). *The Big Leap*. HarperCollins.

23. Sivers, D. (2015). *Derek Sivers on Developing Confidence, Finding Happiness, and Saying "No" to Millions (#125)*. The Tim Ferriss Show. Retrieved on December 6, 2021, at https://tim.blog/2015/12/14/derek-sivers-on-developing-confidence-finding-happiness-and-saying-no-to-millions/

24. Sullivan, D. & Hardy, B. (2020). *Who Not How: The Formula to Achieve Bigger Goals Through Accelerating Teamwork*. Hay House Business.

25. Hendricks, G., & Hendricks, G. (2009). *The Big Leap*. HarperCollins.

26. Sonnentag, S. (2012). Psychological detachment from work during leisure time: The benefits of mentally disengaging from work. *Current Directions in Psychological Science, 21*(2), 114–118.

27. Karabinski, T., Haun, V. C., Nübold, A., Wendsche, J., & Wegge, J. (2021). Interventions for improving psychological detachment from work: A meta-analysis. *Journal of Occupational Health Psychology, 26*(3), 224.

28. Pressfield, S. (2002). *The War of Art: Break Through the Blocks and Win Your Inner Creative Battles*. Black Irish Entertainment LLC.

29. Collins, J. (2001). *Good to Great: Why Some Companies Make the Leap and Others Don't*. HarperBusiness.

30. Ferriss, T. (2014). The Tim Ferriss Show: Interview with Peter Thiel, Billionaire Investor and Company Creator (#28). Retrieved on January 11, 2022, at https://tim.blog/2014/09/09/peter-thiel/

31. Godin, S. (2010). Seth Godin: The Truth About Shipping. 99Designs. Retrieved on January 11, 2022 at https://99u.adobe.com/articles/6249/seth-godin-the-truth-about-shipping

32. Godin, S. (1999). *Permission Marketing: Turning strangers into friends and Friends into Customers*. Simon & Schuster.

33. Godin, S. (2003). *Purple Cow: Transform Your Business by Being rRemarkable*. Portfolio.

34. Godin, S. (2007). *The Dip: A Little Book That Teaches You When to Quit (and When To Stick)*. Portfolio.

35. Godin, S. (2008). *Tribes: We Need You to Lead Us*. Penguin.

36. Grant, A. (2021). *Think Again: The Power of Knowing What You Don't Know*. Viking.

Conclusion

1. Frost, R. (1952). Men of Faith by Philip Hamburger. Start Page 167, Quote Page 169, The New Yorker Magazine Inc., New York. Retrieved on January 13, 2022, at https://quoteinvestigator.com/2020/05/04/bold/

INDEX

A

acceptance, 150–152
Adams, John, 9
adaptation, 28–29
addiction, 88
Adler, Alfred, 2
agency/agency thinking, xx, 12, 115
aggressive completion, 175–181
agricultural stage, 55–56
Allen, James, 152
Apple, 126–128
applied learning, 49
approach motivations/courage, xxiii, xxv, 47–48
Aquino, Benigno, Jr. ("Ninoy"), 62–65
Aquino, Cory, 62–68
Arden, Paul, 7, 44
arena, not being in, 45–50, 107
Aristotle, 69, 70
Art of Asking, The (Palmer), 158–159
Art of Learning, The (Waitzkin), 102
As A Man Thinketh (Allen), 152
asking for what you want, 157–162
Atomic Habits (Clear), 74
attention, selective, xxxvi, 28, 43–44
attitudes
    definite, 73
    indefinite, 73
Auschwitz-Birkenau, 4
automaticity, 103–104
automation, 163–168
avoid motivations/fear, xxiii–xxv
avoidance, 13, 17

B

Barker, Michael, 16
Baumeister, Roy, 9–10
Beatles, 52
beliefs, impact of, 113–121
Bergen-Belsen, 4
Berger, Jonah, 25
Bible, xxxvi, 57, 157
Big Leap, The (Hendricks), 171
blindness, inattentional, 43–44
Brady, Tom, 46
Branson, Richard, 112
Brault, Robert, 54, 111, 141
Brinums, Melissa, 105
Brower, Lee, 187
Buffett, Warren, 51
Butterfly Effect, The, 166

C

Cardone, Grant, 42–43
Carter-Scott, Cherie, 116–117
Cato, 47
change, underestimation of, 78–79
Chapman, Diana, xxxviii, 143–144
Christensen, Clayton, 144
circles, walking in, 97–98
civilization, stages of, 55–56
clarity paradox, 54
Clear, James, 74
Collins, Jim, 132, 174
commitment, xxxviii, 92–94, 143–147, 155, 181
communism, 56–57
completion, aggressive, 175–181
compound effect, 89–90
concentration camps, 3–5, 8, 9, 10, 130
confidence, 90, 181
connection to Future Self
    example of, xxxi–xxxiv
    lack of, 31–36
    quality of, xxvii–xxx
consciousness, map of, 150

context
  creating, 27–28
  mindfulness and, 26
contextual purpose
  clarifying, 129–140
  commitment and, 145
  conflicts with, 146
control, external locus of, 115
costs to Future Self, 86–88
courage/approach, xxiii, xxv, 47–48
Covey, Stephen R., xxxv, 41, 153,
  171–172
creativity, 71–72
crowdfunding, 158
Csikszentmihalyi, Mihaly, 75

D

Dalio, Ray, 57, 179–180
decision fatigue, 166
definite attitudes, 73
deification, 119–120
deliberate practice, 102–105
depression, 115
detachment, 179
detail, 95–100
determinism, xx
Dethmer, Jim, xxxviii, 143–144
Dip, The (Godin), 176–177
discipline, 86
disconnection, 31–36
disengagement thinking, 13
Dispenza, Joe, 151, 171
distractions, 143, 170
Djokovic, Novak, 96
Doctor and the Soul, The (Frankl), 3,
  4–5, 130
Donaldson, Jimmy (MrBeast), xii–
  xix, xxxv, 40, 186–187
donation videos, xv
Dresden Dolls, The, 158–159
Drucker, Peter, 165
Duckworth, Angela, 11, 13, 28
Durant, Ariel, 55–57
Durant, Will, 55–57, 65
Dweck, Carol, 79–80
Dyer, Wayne, 43

E

Eason, Bo, 46
effectiveness, 165
80 Percent Rule, 180–181
Einstein, Albert, 74, 83, 89
Einstein Time, 171
Eisenhower, Dwight D., 40
Emerson, Ralph Waldo, xxxviii, 72
emotional health, 17–18
empathetic witnesses, 17
empathy, 32–33
end-of-history illusion, 79
Entrepreneurial Operating System
  (EOS), 132–133
environment, awareness of, 23–30
Epstein, Brian, 52
Ericsson, Anders, 102–104
evolution, random, 23–30
expectations
  Future Self as different from,
    77–83
  impact of, 24
external locus of control, 115

F

failures
  as Future Self, 101–108
  learning from, 48–49
  success as catalyst for, 51–57
faith, xxxvi, 150, 153
Faulkner, William, 18
fear/avoidance, xxiii–xxv
Ferriss, Tim, 106, 111–112
50 Cent, xxiv, 37
50th Law, The (Greene), xxiv, 37
final cause, 70
fixed mindset, 79–81
flexibility, 82
flow, 75–76
Fogg, BJ, 91
4 freedoms, 170–171
Frankl, Elsa, 2, 3–4
Frankl, Gabriel, 2, 3
Frankl, Viktor
  background of, 2–6

contextual purpose and, 130
Future Self and, xxxi, xxxiv
on goals, 76
hope and, 10–11, 14
purpose and, 8–9, 10–11, 61, 145
on stimulus and response, 27
Franklin, Benjamin, 9
freedoms, four, 170–171
Freud, Sigmund, 2
Frost, Robert, 185
Frumkin, Edward, 102
future
as driver of present, 69–76
pull toward, xx–xxi, xxxvii,
9–10
Future Self Imagination Tool, 83

G

Gaiman, Neil, 142–143
Gap and the Gain, The (Sullivan
and Hardy), 20
Gapingvoid, 177
Gilbert, Daniel, xxix, 77, 78–79,
80–81
goals
12-month, 139–140
breaking down, 75–76, 91
eliminating lesser, 141–147
environments and, 24
flow and, 75–76
hope and, 12
human actions driven by,
xxi–xxii
intelligent action and, 70–71
maturity and, 13
short-term, xxiv, xxvii–xxix, 17
small, 37–44
understanding, xxii–xxiii
God, view of, 113–121
Goddard, Neville, xi
Godin, Seth, 1, 95, 175, 176–178
Goldsmith, Marshall, 26
Good to Great (Collins), 132
Grand Theft Orchestra, 158
Grant, Adam, 179–180
gratitude, 151–152

Greene, Robert, xxiv, 37
grit, 11, 13, 28
Grosser, Tilly, 3–4
growth mindset, 81–82

H

habits, 104
Hardy, Darren, 47
Hawkins, David, xxiii, 47–48, 94,
150
Hendricks, Gay, 52–53, 171
Hershfield, Hal, 32, 33, 35–36
hesitation, 47
high-hope people, 13–14
Hill, Napoleon, 152
Hitler, Adolf, 110–111
Holocaust, 3–5
hope
description of, 11–12
importance of, 7–14
research on, 11, 13
Hopf, G. Michael, 55
Horigome, Yuto, 98–100
Howes, Lewis, 74
Huffington, Arianna, 95
hunting stage, 55–56
Huston, Nyjah, 100

I

identity
actions and, 154–155
commitment and, xxxviii,
92–94
definition of, 152
purpose and, 145
research on, xxv
shift in, 93–94
identity capital, 90
Ignore Everyone (McLeod), 177
imagination, 27, 32, 36, 79–80,
83, 90
imperfect work, completing,
175–181
Imuta, Kana, 105

In Time, 38–39
inattentional blindness, 43–44
indefinite attitudes, 73
industrial stage, 55–56
inevitability thinking, 164
intelligent action/design, 70–72, 73
investing in Future Self, 33–34,
    86–87, 88–94, 133
investment in loss, 102–103,
    104–108
Invisible Influence (Berger), 25
Irenaeus, 119

J

James, William, xxxvi
Jefferson, Thomas, 9
Jobs, Steve, 125, 126–128, 131, 177
Jonas, Regina, 3
Jones, Abner, 120–121
Jones, Charlie, 25

K

Kaufering, 4
King, Martin Luther, Jr., 64
Klemp, Kaley, xxxviii, 143–144
knowing, 149–155
Kotler, Steven, 75

L

Lambert, Nate, 136, 162
Langer, Ellen, 27–28
*Late Show with David Letterman,
    The*, xxviii–xxix
learning, predictions and, xxvii
Lennon, John, 52
Leonardo da Vinci, 178
lesser goals, eliminating, 141–147,
    170, 172–173
Lessons of History, The (Durant and
    Durant), 55–57
letter from Future Self, 36
Letterman, David, xxix

Levine, Peter, 17
Lewis, Alfred Henry, 40
Lewis, C.S., 119–120
life expectancy, xxv
Life Is a Game, These Are the Rules
    (Carter-Scott), 116–117
Linchpin (Godin), 177–178
Livingston, Gordon, 18
logotherapy, 2, 9
Lombardi, Vince, 176–177
long-term planning, 32
loss, investment in, 102–103,
    104–108
low-hope people, 13
Luce, Clare Boothe, 129

M

Man in the Arena, 46
Man's Search for Meaning (Frankl),
    5, 8–9
Marcos, Ferdinand, 62–67
Marcos, Imelda, 63, 67
maturity, explanation of, 13–14
Max Planck Institute for Biological
    Cybernetics, 97
Maxwell, John, 166
McCartney, Paul, 52
McKeown, Greg, 54
McLeod, Hugh, 177
meaning
    importance of, 2–6, 7–14
    past and, 18–19
measureable metrics, 96–97, 100,
    138–139
Mein Kampf (Hitler), 110
Meisel, Ari, 163
memory, 18–19
mere-exposure effect, 25, 28
mindfulness, 26, 27–28
mindsets
    fixed, 79–81
    growth, 81–82
    transactional, 29–30
    transformational, 29–30
Morrow, John, 91
mountain strategy, 142–143

MrBeast (Jimmy Donaldson), xiii–
xix, xxxv, 40, 186–187
multi-tasking, 75–76
Murray, William Hutchinson, 155
myopic decisions, 31–36, 88

N

needing to wanting to knowing,
149–155
Newtonian Time, 171
Nietzsche, Friedrich, 5

O

objectives, clarifying and simplifying, 165
Olson, Jeff, 85
Olympics, 100
optimization, 163
outsourcing, 163
ownership, 17

P

Pagan, Eben, 164
pain
learning from, 19–21
reaction to, 19
Palmer, Amanda, 158–159
Pandolfini, Bruce, 102
Paradox of Choice, The (Schwartz),
166
paralysis-by-analysis, 47, 49, 53, 179
Parkinson's Law, 180
past, reframing, 20
pathology, focus on, xx
pathways thinking, 12, 140
peer groups, 25
perfectionism, 180
Permission Marketing (Godin), 176
Personality Isn't Permanent (Hardy),
136
Phaedo (*On the Soul*; Plato), 70
Philippines, overthrow of Marcos

regime in, 62–68
Picasso, Pablo, 99
pied piper, Future Self as, 85–94
Pixar Studios, 127
Plato, 70
point of no return, 92–94
positive psychologists, xx
post-traumatic growth, 20
Power People Revolution, 67
Powers of Two, The (Shenk), 160
Pressfield, Steven, 110, 173
*Principles for Dealing with the
Changing World Order* (Dalio), 57
Pringles, 88
priorities, 131–140, 166
problems, focus on, xx, 13
procrastination, 173, 180
prospection, xxi, xxv–xxvi, 105
proximity effect, 25
Psychiatric Hospital at the Maria
Theresien Schloessl Neurological Hospital, 3
psychological detachment from
work, 172
psychology, shift in, xix–xx,
xxv–xxvi
Psychology of Your Future Self, The
(Gilbert), 78
Purple Cow (Godin), 176
purpose
clarifying contextual, 129–140
identity and, 145
impact of, 9
loss of, 8
Pygmalion effect, 24, 28

R

reactive behavior, 87–88
reactive narratives, 15–22
regret, 86
resiliency, 5
resistance, 173
Rohn, Jim, 23, 86
Roosevelt, Theodore, 45
Rothschild Hospital, 3
Rumi, 28

S

Saint-Exupéry, Antoine de, 147
scheduling your Future Self,
   169–174
School of Greatness (podcast), 74
Schwartz, Barry, 166
Sculley, John, 127
Searching for Bobby Fischer (Waitz-
   kin), 102
Seinfeld, Jerry, xxviii–xxix
selective attention, xxxvi, 28,
   43–44
self-sabotage, 53
Seligman, Martin, xix
Shadow Careers, 111
Shakespeare, William, 109
Shenk, Joshua Wolf, 160
Shinn, Florence, xxxvi, 150, 153
shipping, 177–179
short-term goals, xxiv, xxvii–xxix
short-term rewards, 34–35
simplification, 126–127, 144
Simpsons, The, xxviii
Sinclair, Bob, 162
Sivers, Derek, 109, 111–112, 169
Slife, Brent, 18–19
Smith, Elias, 120–121
Smith, Joseph, 160–161
Snow, Eliza, 118–119
Snow, Lorenzo, 118
Snyder, Charles, 13
society, failures of, 56–57
sports commentary, 46–47
starting small, 91
Stephen, Graham, 159–160
steps for being your Future Self
   asking for what you want,
      157–162
   automation and systemization,
      163–168
   clarifying contextual purpose,
      129–140
   completing imperfect work,
      175–181
   eliminating lesser goals,
      141–147
   introduction to, 125–128

needing to wanting to knowing,
   149–155
scheduling, 169–174
summary of, 183
stimulus and response, xx, 27
Strategic Coach, 20
Stumbling Upon Happiness (Gilbert),
   78
sub specie aeternitatis, 9, 76
success
   being true to self and, 111–112
   as catalyst for failure, 51–57
   confidence as byproduct of, 90
success disease, 51, 52
Suddendorf, Thomas, 105
suicide rates, Frankl and, 3
Sullivan, Dan, 20, 34, 44, 140, 162,
   165, 170, 180
system design, 164–165, 167
systemization, 163–168

T

Tai Chi, 102
Taiji Push Hands, 102, 104–105
TED Talks, xxvi, 78, 158–159
teleology, xxi, 70
10X Rule, The (Cardone), 42–43
theosis, 119–120
Theresienstadt "Terezin Camp," 3
Thiel, Peter, 72–73, 175
Think Again (Grant), 179
*Those Who Remain: A Postapocalyp-
   tic Novel* (Hopf), 55
threats to Future Self
   disconnection, 31–36
   introduction to, 1–6
   lack of environmental aware-
      ness, 23–30
   lack of hope, 7–14
   not being in the arena, 45–50
   reactive narratives, 15–22
   success disease, 51–57
   summary of, 59
   urgent battles, 37–44
3 Priorities Checklist, 138
Timberlake, Justin, 38

time
  freedom of, 170–173
  as holistic, 18
Time and Psychological Explanation
  (Slife), 18–19
time management, 41
time-capsules, 186–188
Tiny Habits (Fogg), 91
Toy Story, 127
Traction (Wickman), 133
transactional mindset/relation-
  ships, 29–30
transformational mindset/relation-
  ships, 29–30
trauma, 16–17, 21
Tribes (Godin), 177
Triggers (Goldsmith), 26
truths about Future Self
  being true, 109–112
  different from expectations,
    77–83
  failures, 101–108
  future drives the present, 69–76
  introduction to, 61–68
  as pied piper, 85–94
  summary of, 123
  view of God and, 113–121
  vividness and detail, 95–100
Turkheim, 4
Tyson, Mike, 15

U

un-aligning, 29
Universal Tennis Ranking (UTR),
  96–97
upper limit problem, 52–53
urgent battles, 37–44, 170

V

values, importance of, 2
Vienna Neurological Policlinic, 5

vividness, 35–36, 95–100
Vohs, Kathleen, 9–10

W

Waitzkin, Fred, 102
Waitzkin, Josh, 101, 102–103,
  104–107
walking in circles, 97 98
Walsh, Bill, 51
wanting, knowing versus, 149–155
War of Art, The (Pressfield), 110,
  173
Washington, Denzel, 150
Who Not How (Hardy and Sulli-
  van), 136, 165, 170
Wickman, Gino, 132–133
Williams, Serena, 96
Williamson, Marianne, 113
Willpower Doesn't Work (Hardy),
  136
Willson, Meredith, 41
witnesses, empathetic, 17
wolves, reintroduction of, 166–167
Wordsworth, William, 117, 119

X

X-Games, 100

Y

Yellowstone National Park,
  166–167
Yoda, 149
YouTube videos, xii–xix

Z

Ziglar, Zig, 25, 154

(ACKNOWLEDGMENTS)

While writing *Personality Isn't Permanent*, I unexpectedly came across the research on "Future Self." I was immediately gripped and knew I'd one day write a book on the topic. That was almost three years ago from this writing, and the "Future Self" idea has consumed most of my thinking since.

I'd first like to thank and acknowledge all of the researchers and scholars on this new and exciting science. Of particular note are Dr. Marty Seligman, Dr. Roy Baumeister, Dr. Daniel Gilbert, Dr. Hal Hershfield, and Dr. Anders Ericsson.

A huge thanks to Hay House for believing in me and this project. Specifically, thanks to Reid Tracy, Patty Gift, and Melody Guy. Thank you for believing in this project and thank you for your patience as I missed deadline after deadline to get it done. Thank you for your investment in me and my Future Self.

Thanks to Tucker Max for having countless conversations with me about this book over the past 18 months. Thanks for helping me clarify my thinking. Thanks for helping me build my conviction for the importance of this concept. Thanks for challenging me to be my own Future Self, now.

Thanks to Joe Polish for connecting me with Reid Tracy and Tucker Max!

Thanks to my wife, Lauren, and my mom, Susan Knight, for going through draft after draft of this book with me, to help me clarify my thinking and writing. This book would be a mess without your help.

Thanks to PeggySue Wells, for coming onboard the project during the final week of writing and putting your polishing touches on the manuscript. Your little yet important tweaks made this a much better and cleaner book.

Thank you to Gapingvoid for creating the illustratons throughout this book.

To my team, especially Chelsea Jenkins and Natasha Schiffman, for keeping my business thriving while I spent months focused on this project. Thank you for being a part of my team and for loving the work we do. Additional thanks to Meagan Harman, Jenessa Catterson, Alexis Swanson, Kara Avey, Kira Micham, and Katelyn Chadwick.

To everyone who has ever read my blog posts, gone through my online courses, or been a part of my AMP community, thank you for believing in my work. My purpose is to help you clarify and become your best possible Future Selves.

To my family, especially Lauren and my kids: thank you for loving and supporting me. Thank you for the sacrifice and investments you've made that allow me to write these books. I love you very much. You're my #1 priority in my life. I can't wait to continue building and creating our Future Selves together.

To God, thank you for giving me an incredible life. Thank you for your investment in me and my Future Self. Thank you for your grace and gifts. I know that my Future Self will be even more connected to you.

(ABOUT THE AUTHOR)

Dr. Benjamin Hardy is an organizational psychologist, author, and the world's leading expert on the application of the Future Self science. His books have sold hundreds of thousands of copies, and his blogs have been read by hundreds of millions. He and his wife, Lauren, are the parents of six kids. They live in Orlando, Florida.

www.futureself.com

We hope you enjoyed this Hay House book. If you'd like to receive our online catalog featuring additional information on Hay House books and products, or if you'd like to find out more about the Hay Foundation, please contact:

Hay House, Inc., P.O. Box 5100, Carlsbad, CA 92018-5100
(760) 431-7695 or (800) 654-5126
(760) 431-6948 (fax) or (800) 650-5115 (fax)
www.hayhouse.com® • www.hayfoundation.org

———

Published in Australia by: Hay House Australia Pty. Ltd.,
18/36 Ralph St., Alexandria NSW 2015
Phone: 612-9669-4299 • *Fax:* 612-9669-4144
www.hayhouse.com.au

Published in the United Kingdom by: Hay House UK, Ltd.,
The Sixth Floor, Watson House, 54 Baker Street, London W1U 7BU
Phone: +44 (0)20 3927 7290 • *Fax:* +44 (0)20 3927 7291
www.hayhouse.co.uk

Published in India by: Hay House Publishers India,
Muskaan Complex, Plot No. 3, B-2, Vasant Kunj, New Delhi 110 070
Phone: 91-11-4176-1620 • *Fax:* 91-11-4176-1630
www.hayhouse.co.in

———

<u>Access New Knowledge.</u>
<u>Anytime. Anywhere.</u>

Learn and evolve at your own pace
with the world's leading experts.

www.hayhouseU.com